NEW YORK
4th Grade Math
Test Prep

FOR

Common Core
Learning
Standards

teachers' treasures, inc.

Plano, TX

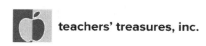

INTRODUCTION

This resource is not intended to be another worksheet to be given to students as a Common Core Learning Standards review. It is the intent of the authors that the questions be used to assess and manage students' understanding of the concepts outlined on the Common Core Standards.

There are at multiple questions for each Common Core Standard. We recommend you create a page made up of questions from various Common Core Standards. The answers can serve as a diagnostic tool to determine WHY the student had an incorrect answer. The answer to the student's misunderstanding is NOT another worksheet, but a re-teaching of the skill, using different instructional strategies.

The reason for incorrect answers is often the result of the student using an incorrect procedure. Most of the errors we see as teachers are the same each year. Students apply a rule in an inappropriate way. Many times they will even say to us, "That's what you said to do." They see logic in the way they have applied the rule even though it is incorrect. Therefore, it is imperative to determine WHY a student chose an incorrect answer to a question. The best way to determine this is to ask the student to explain their reasoning to you.

All questions in this product are aligned to the current Common Core Standards Initiative.

4th Grade
Math Test Prep

FOR

Common Core
Standards

Table of Contents

GRADE 4 MATHEMATICS
COMMON CORE STATE STANDARDS

Operations & Algebraic Thinking	4.OA.1

Interpret a multiplication equation as a comparison, e.g., interpret $35 = 5 \times 7$ as a statement that 35 is 5 times as many as 7 and 7 times as many as 5. Represent verbal statements of multiplicative comparisons as multiplication equations.

Operations & Algebraic Thinking	4.OA.2

Multiply or divide to solve word problems involving multiplicative comparison, e.g., by using drawings and equations with a symbol for the unknown number to represent the problem, distinguishing multiplicative comparison from additive comparison.

Operations & Algebraic Thinking	4.OA.3

Solve multistep word problems posed with whole numbers and having whole-number answers using the four operations, including problems in which remainders must be interpreted. Represent these problems using equations with a letter standing for the unknown quantity. Assess the reasonableness of answers using mental computation and estimation strategies including rounding.

Operations & Algebraic Thinking	4.OA.4

Find all factor pairs for a whole number in the range 1–100. Recognize that a whole number is a multiple of each of its factors. Determine whether a given whole number in the range 1–100 is a multiple of a given one-digit number. Determine whether a given whole number in the range 1–100 is prime or composite.

Operations & Algebraic Thinking	4.OA.5

Generate a number or shape pattern that follows a given rule. Identify apparent features of the pattern that were not explicit in the rule itself. *For example, given the rule "Add 3" and the starting number 1, generate terms in the resulting sequence and observe that the terms appear to alternate between odd and even numbers. Explain informally why the numbers will continue to alternate in this way.*

Number & Operations in Base Ten   4.NBT.1

Recognize that in a multi-digit whole number, a digit in one place represents ten times what it represents in the place to its right. *For example, recognize that 700 ÷ 70 = 10 by applying concepts of place value and division.*

Number & Operations in Base Ten   4.NBT.2

Read and write multi-digit whole numbers using base-ten numerals, number names, and expanded form. Compare two multi-digit numbers based on meanings of the digits in each place, using >, =, and < symbols to record the results of comparisons.

Number & Operations in Base Ten   4.NBT.3

Use place value understanding to round multi-digit whole numbers to any place.

Number & Operations in Base Ten   4.NBT.4

Fluently add and subtract multi-digit whole numbers using the standard algorithm.

Number & Operations in Base Ten   4.NBT.5

Multiply a whole number of up to four digits by a one-digit whole number, and multiply two two-digit numbers, using strategies based on place value and the properties of operations. Illustrate and explain the calculation by using equations, rectangular arrays, and/or area models.

Number & Operations in Base Ten   4.NBT.6

Find whole-number quotients and remainders with up to four-digit dividends and one-digit divisors, using strategies based on place value, the properties of operations, and/or the relationship between multiplication and division. Illustrate and explain the calculation by using equations, rectangular arrays, and/or area models.

Number & Operations - Fractions   4.NF.1

Explain why a fraction a/b is equivalent to a fraction $(n \times a)/(n \times b)$ by using visual fraction models, with attention to how the number and size of the parts differ even though the two fractions themselves are the same size. Use this principle to recognize and generate equivalent fractions.

Number & Operations - Fractions — 4.NF.2

Compare two fractions with different numerators and different denominators, e.g., by creating common denominators or numerators, or by comparing to a benchmark fraction such as 1/2. Recognize that comparisons are valid only when the two fractions refer to the same whole. Record the results of comparisons with symbols >, =, or <, and justify the conclusions, e.g., by using a visual fraction model.

Number & Operations - Fractions — 4.NF.3

Understand a fraction a/b with $a > 1$ as a sum of fractions $1/b$. Understand addition and subtraction of fractions as joining and separating parts referring to the same whole. Decompose a fraction into a sum of fractions with the same denominator in more than one way, recording each decomposition by an equation. Justify decompositions, e.g., by using a visual fraction model. *Examples: 3/8 = 1/8 + 1/8 + 1/8 ; 3/8 = 1/8 + 2/8 ; 2 1/8 = 1 + 1 + 1/8 = 8/8 + 8/8 + 1/8.* Add and subtract mixed numbers with like denominators, e.g., by replacing each mixed number with an equivalent fraction, and/or by using properties of operations and the relationship between addition and subtraction. Solve word problems involving addition and subtraction of fractions referring to the same whole and having like denominators, e.g., by using visual fraction models and equations to represent the problem.

Number & Operations - Fractions — 4.NF.4

Apply and extend previous understandings of multiplication to multiply a fraction by a whole number. Understand a fraction a/b as a multiple of $1/b$. *For example, use a visual fraction model to represent 5/4 as the product 5 × (1/4), recording the conclusion by the equation 5/4 = 5 × (1/4).* Understand a multiple of a/b as a multiple of 1/b, and use this understanding to multiply a fraction by a whole number. *For example, use a visual fraction model to express 3 × (2/5) as 6 × (1/5), recognizing this product as 6/5. (In general, n × (a/b) = (n × a)/b.).* Solve word problems involving multiplication of a fraction by a whole number, e.g., by using visual fraction models and equations to represent the problem. *For example, if each person at a party will eat 3/8 of a pound of roast beef, and there will be 5 people at the party, how many pounds of roast beef will be needed? Between what two whole numbers does your answer lie?*

Number & Operations - Fractions   4.NF.5

Express a fraction with denominator 10 as an equivalent fraction with denominator 100, and use this technique to add two fractions with respective denominators 10 and 100.[2] *For example, express 3/10 as 30/100, and add 3/10 + 4/100 = 34/100.*

Number & Operations - Fractions   4.NF.6

Use decimal notation for fractions with denominators 10 or 100. *For example, rewrite 0.62 as 62/100; describe a length as 0.62 meters; locate 0.62 on a number line diagram.*

Number & Operations - Fractions   4.NF.7

Compare two decimals to hundredths by reasoning about their size. Recognize that comparisons are valid only when the two decimals refer to the same whole. Record the results of comparisons with the symbols >, =, or <, and justify the conclusions, e.g., by using a visual model.

Measurement & Data   4.MD.1

Know relative sizes of measurement units within one system of units including km, m, cm; kg, g; lb, oz.; l, ml; hr, min, sec. Within a single system of measurement, express measurements in a larger unit in terms of a smaller unit. Record measurement equivalents in a two-column table. *For example, know that 1 ft is 12 times as long as 1 in. Express the length of a 4 ft snake as 48 in. Generate a conversion table for feet and inches listing the number pairs (1, 12), (2, 24), (3, 36), ...*

Measurement & Data   4.MD.2

Use the four operations to solve word problems involving distances, intervals of time, liquid volumes, masses of objects, and money, including problems involving simple fractions or decimals, and problems that require expressing measurements given in a larger unit in terms of a smaller unit. Represent measurement quantities using diagrams such as number line diagrams that feature a measurement scale.

Measurement & Data   4.MD.3

Apply the area and perimeter formulas for rectangles in real world and mathematical problems. *For example, find the width of a rectangular room given the area of the flooring and the length, by viewing the area formula as a multiplication equation with an unknown factor.*

Measurement & Data   4.MD.4

Make a line plot to display a data set of measurements in fractions of a unit (1/2, 1/4, 1/8). Solve problems involving addition and subtraction of fractions by using information presented in line plots. *For example, from a line plot find and interpret the difference in length between the longest and shortest specimens in an insect collection.*

Measurement & Data   4.MD.5

Recognize angles as geometric shapes that are formed wherever two rays share a common endpoint, and understand concepts of angle measurement: An angle is measured with reference to a circle with its center at the common endpoint of the rays, by considering the fraction of the circular arc between the points where the two rays intersect the circle. An angle that turns through 1/360 of a circle is called a "one-degree angle," and can be used to measure angles. An angle that turns through n one-degree angles is said to have an angle measure of n degrees.

Measurement & Data   4.MD.6

Measure angles in whole-number degrees using a protractor. Sketch angles of specified measure.

Measurement & Data   4.MD.7

Recognize angle measure as additive. When an angle is decomposed into non-overlapping parts, the angle measure of the whole is the sum of the angle measures of the parts. Solve addition and subtraction problems to find unknown angles on a diagram in real world and mathematical problems, e.g., by using an equation with a symbol for the unknown angle measure.

Geometry   4.G.1

Draw points, lines, line segments, rays, angles (right, acute, obtuse), and perpendicular and parallel lines. Identify these in two-dimensional figures.

Geometry   4.G.2

Classify two-dimensional figures based on the presence or absence of parallel or perpendicular lines, or the presence or absence of angles of a specified size. Recognize right triangles as a category, and identify right triangles.

Geometry   4.G.3

Recognize a line of symmetry for a two-dimensional figure as a line across the figure such that the figure can be folded along the line into matching parts. Identify line-symmetric figures and draw lines of symmetry.

Grade 4
Mathematics Chart

LENGTH

Metric

1 kilometer = 1000 meters
1 meter = 100 centimeters
1 centimeter = 10 millimeters

Customary

1 yard = 3 feet
1 yard = 3 feet
1 foot = 12 inches

CAPACITY & VOLUME

Metric

1 liter = 1000 milliliters

Customary

1 gallon = 4 quarts
1 gallon = 128 ounces
1 quart = 2 pints
1 pint = 2 cups
1 cup = 8 ounces

MASS & WEIGHT

Metric

1 kilogram = 1000 grams
1 gram = 1000 milligrams

Customary

1 ton = 2000 pounds
1 pound = 16 ounces

TIME

1 year = 365 days

1 year = 12 months

1 year = 52 weeks

1 week = 7 days

1 day = 24 hours

1 hour = 60 minutes

1 minute = 60 seconds

Common Core Standard 4.OA.1 – Operations & Algebraic Thinking

☐   Jason has 4 times as many baseball cards as Brandon. Brandon has 8 cards. How many cards does Jason have?

(A)   32

(B)   36

(C)   28

(D)   12

Common Core Standard 4.OA.1 – Operations & Algebraic Thinking

☐   Yolanda walks 3 miles each week. She rides her bicycle 4 miles a week. How many miles will she walk in 4 weeks?

(A)   7

(B)   11

(C)   12

(D)   16

Common Core Standard 4.OA.1 – Operations & Algebraic Thinking

☐   Which is the product of $7 \times (4 \times 2)$?

(A)   14

(B)   28

(C)   27

(D)   56

Common Core Standard 4.OA.1 – Operations & Algebraic Thinking

☐   **Which multiplication problem has a product of 96?**

(A)   90 + 6

(B)   12 × 8

(C)   9 × 10

(D)   (3 × 2) × 9

Common Core Standard 4.OA.1 – Operations & Algebraic Thinking

☐   **A pencil company packs 10 pencils in a box and 4 boxes in a carton. A school has ordered 3 cartons. Which number sentence could you use to find the total number of pencils the school ordered?**

(A)   10 × (4 × 3)

(B)   (4 + 3) × 10

(C)   10 + 4 + 3

(D)   14 × 3

Common Core Standard 4.OA.1 – Operations & Algebraic Thinking

☐   **Jade has a new photo album that has twelve pages in it. She can place 9 pictures on each page. How many pictures will fill all of the pages in the album?**

(A)   21

(B)   96

(C)   108

(D)   98

Name _____   Date_____

Common Core Standard 4.OA.1 – Operations & Algebraic Thinking

[ ] **Victoria eats 5 slices of bread and drinks 8 glasses of water each day. How many slices of bread does she eat in a 7 day week?**

(A) 56

(B) 91

(C) 12

(D) 35

Common Core Standard 4.OA.1 – Operations & Algebraic Thinking

[ ] **Which is the product of $(3 \times 3) \times 9$?**

(A) 54

(B) 27

(C) 81

(D) 72

Common Core Standard 4.OA.1 – Operations & Algebraic Thinking

[ ] **Which multiplication problem has a product of 64?**

(A) 8×8

(B) $50 + 14$

(C) 8×7

(D) 6×10

Common Core Standard 4.OA.1 – Operations & Algebraic Thinking

☐ The flower arrangements on the tables in a restaurant have 7 flowers in each of them. There are 5 tables in one eating area and 6 tables in the outside eating area. Which number sentence would show how many flowers were used in all of the arrangements?

(A) 7 + 5 + 6

(B) 5 × 6

(C) (5 + 6) × 7

(D) 7 × 10

Common Core Standard 4.OA.1 – Operations & Algebraic Thinking

☐ Jacob does 9 abdominal crunches in PE every day of the school week. How many crunches does he do in one school week?

(A) 9

(B) 36

(C) 63

(D) 45

Common Core Standard 4.OA.1 – Operations & Algebraic Thinking

☐ Each girl in a scout troop sold 15 boxes of chocolate cookies and 11 boxes of pecan cookies. There are 12 girls in the scout troop. How many boxes of pecan cookies did they sell?

(A) 232

(B) 132

(C) 38

(D) 23

Common Core Standard 4.OA.1 – Operations & Algebraic Thinking

☐ **Which is the product of 6 × (4 × 3)?**

Ⓐ 72

Ⓑ 42

Ⓒ 24

Ⓓ 18

Common Core Standard 4.OA.1 – Operations & Algebraic Thinking

☐ **Which multiplication problem has a product of 144?**

Ⓐ (9 × 7) × 2

Ⓑ (9 × 9) × 3

Ⓒ 12 × (4 × 3)

Ⓓ 12 + (4 × 3)

Common Core Standard 4.OA.1 – Operations & Algebraic Thinking

☐ **For his 9th birthday Trent received a card from each of his 2 grandmothers. Each grandmother put $5 in the card. Which number sentence shows how much money Trent received on his birthday from his grandmothers?**

Ⓐ 2 + 5

Ⓑ 2 + 5 + 9

Ⓒ (2 × 5) × 9

Ⓓ 2 × 5

Common Core Standard 4.OA.1 – Operations & Algebraic Thinking

☐ If 6 times a number is 30, which expression could be used to find the number?

(A) 30 + 6

(B) 30 − 6

(C) 30 × 6

(D) 30 ÷ 6

Common Core Standard 4.OA.1 – Operations & Algebraic Thinking

☐ Which number sentence is in the same family of facts as 21 ÷ 7 = 3?

(A) 21 − 7 = 14

(B) 7 × 3 = 21

(C) 7 + 3 = 10

(D) 21 × 7 = 147

Common Core Standard 4.OA.1 – Operations & Algebraic Thinking

☐ One of the number sentences in the box does not belong with the others. Which number sentence is it?

(A) 9 × 4 = 36

(B) 36 ÷ 4 = 9

(C) 9 + 4 = 13

(D) 36 ÷ 9 = 4

| 9 x 4 = 36 |
| 9 + 4 = 13 |
| 36 ÷ 4 = 9 |
| 36 ÷ 9 = 4 |

Name _____   Date_____

Common Core Standard 4.OA.2 – Operations & Algebraic Thinking

☐   A florist delivered 30 flower arrangements on Friday. The arrangements cost $15 each. Each arrangement held 25 flowers. Which number sentence could be used to find the total number of flowers used in the arrangements?

(A) $30 + \$15 = $ ☐

(B) $25 \times 30 \times \$15 = $ ☐

(C) $30 \times 25 = $ ☐

(D) $30 \div \$15 = $ ☐

Common Core Standard 4.OA.2 – Operations & Algebraic Thinking

☐   Andrew has 92 pennies. He wants to put them into 8 boxes. If he puts the same number of pennies in each box, which number sentence could be used to find the number of pennies that will be in each box?

(A) $92 + 8 = $ ☐

(B) $92 \times 8 = $ ☐

(C) $92 - 8 = $ ☐

(D) $92 \div 8 = $ ☐

Common Core Standard 4.OA.2 – Operations & Algebraic Thinking

☐   The graph shows the number of pencils 5 students in Ms. Granger's class have in their desks. Who had 3 times as many pencils as Angie?

(A)   Sarah

(B)   Ricardo

(C)   Julietta

(D)   Gavin

Name _____   Date_____

Common Core Standard 4.OA.2 – Operations & Algebraic Thinking

☐   A snow cone stand is open 7 days a week. Last week it sold 88 snow cones each day. Which number sentence could be used to find the number of snow cones sold last week?

(A)   88 ÷ 7 = ☐

(B)   88 + 7 = ☐

(C)   88 × 7 = ☐

(D)   88 − 7 = ☐

Common Core Standard 4.OA.2 – Operations & Algebraic Thinking

☐   The graph shows the number of computers that have been placed in different rooms in an intermediate school. Use the graph to answer the questions below.

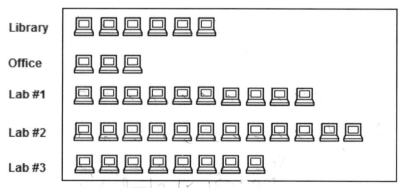

Each 🖥 means 3 computers.

☐ How many computers are is located in the office and lab #3?

(A)   11

(B)   33

(C)   39

(D)   17

☐ If each computer in lab #1 used 5 times a day, how Many times are the computers in lab #1 used in all?

(A)   50

(B)   15

(C)   6

(D)   150

Common Core Standard 4.OA.2 – Operations & Algebraic Thinking

☐ Mrs. Rogers canned 40 cans of tomatoes last summer. She put the cans on shelves with the same number on each shelf. Which arrangement would NOT be possible if she put all of the cans of tomatoes on the shelves?

(A) 5 shelves of 8 cans

(B) 4 shelves of 10 cans

(C) 8 shelves of 6 cans

(D) 2 shelves of 20 cans

Common Core Standard 4.OA.2 – Operations & Algebraic Thinking

☐ The picture shows stacks of pennies. Which number sentence represents the way the pennies are stacked?

(A) 6 × 4 = 24   (C) 28 – 4 = 24

(B) 28 ÷ 4 = 7   (D) 28 – 7 = 21

Common Core Standard 4.OA.2 – Operations & Algebraic Thinking

☐ A hobby club meets 20 times a year. The 35 members pay $22 a year in dues to belong to the club. Which number sentence could be used to find the total amount of money paid in dues for a year?

(A) 35 + $22 = ☐

(B) 20 × $22 = ☐

(C) 35 + $22 + 20 = ☐

(D) 35 × $22 = ☐

Name _____   Date_____

Common Core Standard 4.OA.2 – Operations & Algebraic Thinking

☐ A factory made 1,500 footballs over a period of 15 days. If the same number of footballs were made each day, which number sentence could be used to find how many footballs were made in one day?

(A) 1,500 + 15 = ☐

(B) 1,500 ÷ 15 = ☐

(C) 1,500 − 15 = ☐

(D) 1,500 × 15 = ☐

Common Core Standard 4.OA.2 – Operations & Algebraic Thinking

☐ The graph shows the number of balls a coach ordered for the new school year. Which kind of ball did the coach order twice as many of as soccer balls?

(A) Baseballs

(B) Volleyballs

(C) Footballs

(D) Basketballs

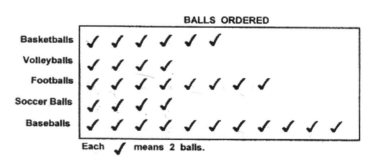

Common Core Standard 4.OA.2 – Operations & Algebraic Thinking

☐ Hector found 22 seashells on a beach. His brothers found 3 times as many as he did. Which number sentence could be used to find the number of seashells his brothers found?

(A) ☐ ÷ 3 = 22

(B) 22 + 3 = ☐

(C) 22 − ☐ = 3

(D) 22 × 3 = ☐

Name _____   Date_____

Common Core Standard 4.OA.2 – Operations & Algebraic Thinking

☐ The graph shows the results of a survey of fourth grade students to find their favorite flavor of ice cream. Use the graph to answer the questions below.

FAVORITE ICE CREAM FLAVORS

Vanilla	🍦🍦🍦🍦🍦🍦🍦
Chocolate	🍦🍦🍦🍦🍦🍦🍦🍦🍦🍦🍦🍦🍦
Strawberry	🍦🍦🍦🍦🍦🍦🍦🍦🍦
Lemon	🍦🍦🍦🍦🍦
Cherry	🍦🍦

Each 🍦 means 3 votes.

☐ How many students chose chocolate as their favorite flavor?

(A) 13

(B) 26

(C) 39

(D) 36

☐ If each student that chose cherry as their favorite flavor ate 6 cones each week, how many cones would they eat in one week?

(A) 8

(B) 36

(C) 12

(D) 42

Common Core Standard 4.OA.2 – Operations & Algebraic Thinking

☐ The picture shows stacks of quarters. Which number sentence represents the way the quarters are grouped?

     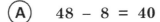 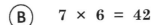

(A) 48 − 8 = 40

(B) 7 × 6 = 42

(C) 48 ÷ 8 = 6

(D) 8 + 6 = 14

Common Core Standard 4.OA.2 – Operations & Algebraic Thinking

☐ A music club sold apples at lunch each day to raise money to buy a new piano. The club sold a total of 108 apples. If they sold the same number of apples each day, which of the following would NOT be possible?

(A) 3 days selling 36 apples each day

(B) 4 days selling 27 apples each day

(C) 9 days selling 12 apples each day

(D) 10 days selling 10 apples each day

Common Core Standard 4.OA.2 – Operations & Algebraic Thinking

☐ There are 14 fourth grade classes and 11 third grade classes at Brooks Intermediate. Each fourth grade class has 24 students. Which number sentence could be used to find the total number of students in the fourth grade?

(A) $14 + 11 + 24 = \square$

(B) $14 \times 24 = \square$

(C) $24 \div 14 = \square$

(D) $11 \times 24 = \square$

Common Core Standard 4.OA.2 – Operations & Algebraic Thinking

☐ A football team scored 217 points in 7 games. If they scored the same number of points in each game, which number sentence could be used to find the number of points they scored in each game?

(A) $217 \div 7 = \square$

(B) $217 + 7 = \square$

(C) $217 \times 7 = \square$

(D) $217 - 7 = \square$

Name _____   Date_____

Common Core Standard 4.OA.3 – Operations & Algebraic Thinking

☐ **What information is needed to solve the following problem?**

> Mr. Rogers bought fencing for his yard. He needs to cut it into 9 equal pieces. He will have 3 feet left over when he finishes the job. How long will each piece of fencing be?

(A) When Mr. Rogers bought the fencing

(B) What kind of fencing Mr. Rogers bought

(C) How much fencing he bought

(D) No more information is needed.

Common Core Standard 4.OA.3 – Operations & Algebraic Thinking

☐ **What do you need to do to solve this problem?**

> Brandon wants to buy tires for his three-wheeler. They will cost a total of $27. How much will 1 tire cost?

(A) Divide $27 by 3

(B) Divide $27 by 4

(C) Add $27 and 3

(D) Multiply $27 by 3

Common Core Standard 4.OA.3 – Operations & Algebraic Thinking

☐ **Mr. Richards bought two 3 liter bottles of soda for the class party. There are 16 students in his class. If all of the students receive equal amounts of soda, how many liters of soda will 8 students receive?**

(A) 4 liters

(B) 3 liters

(C) 6 liters

(D) 48 liters

Common Core Standard 4.OA.3 – Operations & Algebraic Thinking

☐ Ricardo bought a package of 59 suckers to share with his friends. He gave each of his 6 friends an equal number of suckers and had 5 left in the package. How many suckers did he give to each friend?

(A) 7

(B) 8

(C) 10

(D) 9

Common Core Standard 4.OA.3 – Operations & Algebraic Thinking

☐ Reid has collected 616 pennies that he wants to put into 4 different piggy banks. If he puts the same amount of pennies in each bank, how many pennies will be in each bank?

(A) 612

(B) 2,464

(C) 154

(D) 620

Common Core Standard 4.OA.3 – Operations & Algebraic Thinking

☐ What is the remainder when 19 is divided by 4?

(A) 3

(B) 4

(C) 5

(D) 23

Common Core Standard 4.OA.3 – Operations & Algebraic Thinking

☐ A PTA is sponsoring a garage sale. There will be 48 tables of sale items. Each classroom will have 7 tables of items. What is the largest number of classrooms that can participate in the garage sale?

(A) 56

(B) 6

(C) 8

(D) 7

Common Core Standard 4.OA.3 – Operations & Algebraic Thinking

☐ Benjamin has 89 stamps. His book has 8 pages. If he puts an equal number of stamps on each page in his book, how many stamps will he put on each page?

(A) 81

(B) 9

(C) 10

(D) 11

Common Core Standard 4.OA.3 – Operations & Algebraic Thinking

☐ Matthew's family visited an amusement park last summer. Each member of his family rode 7 rides. They stayed at the park for 6 hours. If they rode a total of 63 rides, how many people are in Matthew's family?

(A) 8

(B) 70

(C) 9

(D) 9 R2

Name _____   Date_____

Common Core Standard 4.OA.3 – Operations & Algebraic Thinking

☐ Hailey bought 3 bags of oranges and 2 bags of apples. The oranges cost $1.50, and the apples cost $0.98. Which number sentence could be used to find how much each bag of oranges costs?

(A) $1.50 × 3 = ☐

(B) $1.50 ÷ 3 = ☐

(C) $1.50 + 3 = ☐

(D) $0.98 ÷ 3 = ☐

Common Core Standard 4.OA.3 – Operations & Algebraic Thinking

☐ Nicole wants to buy a new video game. The recycling center pays 30¢ per pound for cans. What other information is needed to determine the number of pounds she needs to collect to have enough money to buy the video game?

(A)   The name of the video game

(B)   The kinds of cans she will collect

(C)   How long she will collect the cans

(D)   The cost of the video game

Common Core Standard 4.OA.3 – Operations & Algebraic Thinking

☐ What do you need to do to solve this problem?

> Mr. Espinosa gave some of the students in his class 3 pencils each for perfect attendance. If he passed out a total of 36 pencils, how many students had perfect attendance?

(A)   Subtract 3 from 36

(B)   Divide 36 by 3

(C)   Add 36 and 3

(D)   Multiply 36 by 3

Common Core Standard 4.OA.3 – Operations & Algebraic Thinking

☐ Brad rode his bicycle a total of 63 miles last week. This week he has ridden his bike 42 miles. If he rode the same number of miles every day, how many miles did he ride each day last week?

(A) 9 miles

(B) 6 miles

(C) 15 miles

(D) 8 miles

Common Core Standard 4.OA.3 – Operations & Algebraic Thinking

☐ Mr. Zamora bought 28 shrubs to plant at his new house. He wanted to plant an equal number of shrubs in 6 different flowerbeds. When he finished planting the shrubs, he had 4 left over. How many shrubs did he plant in each flowerbed?

(A) 3

(B) 4

(C) 5

(D) 6

Common Core Standard 4.OA.3 – Operations & Algebraic Thinking

☐ Betsy likes to read books about horses. She reads 3 books a week. How many weeks will it take her to read 24 books?

(A) 7

(B) 7 R2

(C) 8

(D) 8 R3

Common Core Standard 4.OA.3 – Operations & Algebraic Thinking

☐ **What is the remainder when 43 is divided by 5?**

Ⓐ 2

Ⓑ 3

Ⓒ 48

Ⓓ 4

Common Core Standard 4.OA.3 – Operations & Algebraic Thinking

☐ **Ms. Maybrey collects coins for a hobby. She has collected 83 coins over the years.   If she puts her coins in display pages, she can create a book filled with her coins. Each page will hold 8 coins. What is the least number of pages Ms. Maybrey needs to buy for her book without having any pages left over?**

Ⓐ 11

Ⓑ 10

Ⓒ 91

Ⓓ 12

Common Core Standard 4.OA.3 – Operations & Algebraic Thinking

☐ **A bakery baked 112 cookies that need to put into 9 sacks. They will put an equal number of cookies in each sack. How many cookies will be placed in each sack?**

Ⓐ 11

Ⓑ 103

Ⓒ 12

Ⓓ 12

Common Core Standard 4.OA.4 – Operations & Algebraic Thinking

☐   **Which numbers in the list below are prime numbers?**

1   2   4   8

(A)   4

(B)   1

(C)   2

(D)   8

Common Core Standard 4.OA.4 – Operations & Algebraic Thinking

☐   **Which numbers in the list below are prime numbers?**

7   9   10   15

(A)   7

(B)   15

(C)   10

(D)   9

Common Core Standard 4.OA.4 – Operations & Algebraic Thinking

☐   **Which numbers in the list below are prime numbers?**

22   47   63   75

(A)   63

(B)   22

(C)   47

(D)   75

Common Core Standard 4.OA.4 – Operations & Algebraic Thinking

☐   **Which numbers in the list below are prime numbers?**

81   92   105 113

(A)   105

(B)   81

(C)   113

(D)   92

Common Core Standard 4.OA.4 – Operations & Algebraic Thinking

☐   **Which numbers in the list below are prime numbers?**

281 197 163 501

(A)   163

(B)   501

(C)   281

(D)   197

Common Core Standard 4.OA.4 – Operations & Algebraic Thinking

☐   **Which numbers in the list below are prime numbers?**

1473 2178 521 4565

(A)   1473

(B)   521

(C)   4565

(D)   2178

Name _____   Date_____

Common Core Standard 4.OA.4 – Operations & Algebraic Thinking

⬜ **Choose the correct factor set for the number below?**

8

(A)   1, 2, 4

(B)   2, 4, 6, 8

(C)   1, 2, 4, 6

(D)   1, 2, 4, 8

Common Core Standard 4.OA.4 – Operations & Algebraic Thinking

⬜ **Choose the correct factor set for the number below?**

14

(A)   2, 4, 6, 8

(B)   1, 2, 7, 14

(C)   1, 2, 7

(D)   1, 2, 7, 12

⬜ **Choose the correct factor set for the number below?**

10

(A)   1, 2, 5, 10

(B)   1, 2, 5

(C)   1, 2, 5, 8

(D)   2, 4, 6, 8

Common Core Standard 4.OA.4 – Operations & Algebraic Thinking

☐   **Choose the correct factor set for the number below?**

27

- (A)   1, 3, 9
- (B)   1, 3, 5, 7
- (C)   1, 3, 9, 27
- (D)   1, 3, 9, 11

Common Core Standard 4.OA.4 – Operations & Algebraic Thinking

☐   **Choose the correct factor set for the number below?**

17

- (A)   1, 17
- (B)   1, 3, 5, 7
- (C)   1, 3, 7
- (D)   3, 17

☐   **Choose the correct factor set for the number below?**

21

- (A)   3, 7, 11
- (B)   1, 3, 7, 21
- (C)   1, 3, 7
- (D)   1, 3, 5, 7

Common Core Standard 4.OA.4 – Operations & Algebraic Thinking

☐   **Choose the correct factor set for the number below?**

22

Ⓐ   2, 4, 6, 11

Ⓑ   1, 2, 11

Ⓒ   1, 2, 11, 22

Ⓓ   2, 4, 6, 8

Common Core Standard 4.OA.4 – Operations & Algebraic Thinking

☐   **Choose the correct factor set for the number below?**

52

Ⓐ   1, 2, 4, 13, 26, 52

Ⓑ   1, 2, 4, 12, 26, 52

Ⓒ   1, 52

Ⓓ   2, 4, 6, 8

☐   **Choose the correct factor set for the number below?**

90

Ⓐ   1, 3, 9, 10, 30

Ⓑ   2, 3, 5, 7, 11, 13, 17

Ⓒ   1, 3, 5, 7, 9, 10, 15, 18, 45, 90

Ⓓ   1, 2, 3, 5, 6, 9, 10, 15, 18, 45, 90

Name _____   Date_____

Common Core Standard 4.OA.5 – Operations & Algebraic Thinking

☐   Darrell works at a car wash on the weekends. The table shows how many cars can be washed and vacuumed in 3, 5, and 7 hours. If the car wash is open 10 hours on the weekends, how many cars can be cleaned?

Ⓐ   180

Ⓑ   200

Ⓒ   280

Ⓓ   160

Number of Cars	Number of Hours
60	3
100	5
140	7

Common Core Standard 4.OA.5 – Operations & Algebraic Thinking

☐   Goody Candy Company sells candy by the bag. The table shows how many pieces of candy are in 2, 5, and 9 bags. If the company sells 25 bags to Moore's Grocery, how many pieces of candy will the grocery store buy?

Ⓐ   250

Ⓑ   1000

Ⓒ   2,500

Ⓓ   2,000

Number of Bags	Number of Candy Pieces
2	200
5	500
9	900

Common Core Standard 4.OA.5 – Operations & Algebraic Thinking

☐   Franklin and his friend have a paper route. The table shows the number of newspapers they can fold and wrap in 2, 6, and 9 minutes. Which expression can be used to find how many newspapers Franklin and his friend can fold and wrap in 30 minutes?

Ⓐ $30 \div 10$

Ⓑ 30×60

Ⓒ $30 + 10$

Ⓓ 30×10

Number of Newspapers	Number of Minutes
20	2
60	6
90	9

Name _____   Date_____

☐   The table shows how many airplanes land in 5, 8, and 15 minutes at a busy airport in Texas. Which expression can be used to find how many airplanes land at the airport in 45 minutes?

(A)   45 × 100

(B)   45 × 60

(C)   45 + 100

(D)   45 ÷ 10

Number of Airplanes	Number of Minutes
500	5
800	8
1500	15

☐   The table shows how many vehicles pass through a tollbooth on an expressway in 2, 6, and 9 hours. If the pattern continues, how many vehicles will pass through the tollbooth in 18 hours?

(A)   130

(B)   1,800

(C)   180

(D)   100

Number of Vehicles	Number of Hours
20	2
60	6
90	9

☐   The table shows the number of passengers who can ride 4, 9, and 12 city buses each week. If the pattern continues, how many passengers can ride 22 buses?

(A)   1,300

(B)   2,200

(C)   2,000

(D)   220

Number of Buses	Number of Passengers
4	400
9	900
12	1200

Common Core Standard 4.OA.5 – Operations & Algebraic Thinking

☐   The table shows how many award ribbons are packed in 4, 7, and 8 boxes. Which expression can be used to find how many award ribbons are in 25 boxes?

Ⓐ   25 + 10

Ⓑ   25 × 100

Ⓒ   25 × 10

Ⓓ   25 ÷ 10

Number of Ribbons	Number of Boxes
40	4
70	7
80	8

Common Core Standard 4.OA.5 – Operations & Algebraic Thinking

☐   Mrs. Mason uses small safety pins when she makes Christmas decorations. The table shows how many small safety pins are in 3, 5, and 8 packages. Which expression can be used to find how many small safety pins are in 14 packages?

Ⓐ   14 + 100

Ⓑ   14 × 100

Ⓒ   14 × 10

Ⓓ   14 ÷ 100

Number of Packages	Number of Pins
3	300
5	500
8	800

Common Core Standard 4.OA.5 – Operations & Algebraic Thinking

☐   Mr. Boone uses colored paper when he prints menus for his restaurant. The table shows how many sheets of paper are in 4, 7, and 11 packages. If Mr. Boone used 16 packages of colored paper this week, how many sheets of colored paper did he use?

Ⓐ   120

Ⓑ   26

Ⓒ   500

Ⓓ   160

Number of Packages	Number of Sheets
4	40
7	70
11	110

Name _____   Date_____

Common Core Standard 4.OA.5 – Operations & Algebraic Thinking

☐   The table shows how many cookies are packaged in 3, 7, and 13 boxes. If the pattern continues, how many cookies are packaged in 35 boxes?

(A) 35,000

(B) 48

(C) 350

(D) 3,500

Number of Boxes	Number of Cookies
3	300
7	700
13	1300

Common Core Standard 4.OA.5 – Operations & Algebraic Thinking

☐   Which pair of numbers best completes the equation?

$$\boxed{} \times 100 = \bigcirc$$

(A) 240 and 2,400   (C) 24 and 240

(B) 24 and 2,400   (D) 204 and 2,004

Common Core Standard 4.OA.5 – Operations & Algebraic Thinking

☐   The table shows how many labels are packaged in 2, 4, and 7 boxes. Which expression can be used to find how many labels are in 33 boxes?

(A) 33 × 10

(B) 33 + 10

(C) 33 × 100

(D) 33 ÷ 10

Number of Boxes	Number of Labels
2	200
4	400
7	700

Name _____   **Date** _____

Common Core Standard 4.OA.5 – Operations & Algebraic Thinking

☐   **Which pair of numbers best completes the equation?**

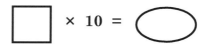

(A) ☐ 103 and ⬭ 1,300   (C) ☐ 13 and ⬭ 130

(B) ☐ 13 and ⬭ 1,300   (D) ☐ 130 and ⬭ 130

Common Core Standard 4.OA.5 – Operations & Algebraic Thinking

☐   **Mr. Baker saves old coins. The table shows how many old coins can be placed in 5, 11, and 13 boxes. Which expression can be used to find how many old coins Mr. Baker has saved if he has 24 boxes of old coins?**

(A) 24 + 10

(B) 24 × 10

(C) 24 × 100

(D) 24 ÷ 10

Number of Boxes	Number of Coins
5	50
11	110
13	130

Common Core Standard 4.OA.5 – Operations & Algebraic Thinking

☐   **Which pair of numbers best completes the equation?**

☐ × 100 = ⬭

(A) ☐ 55 and ⬭ 550   (C) ☐ 505 and ⬭ 5,050

(B) ☐ 550 and ⬭ 5,005   (D) ☐ 55 and ⬭ 5,500

Common Core Standard 4.NBT.1 – Numbers & Operations in Base Ten

☐   **What is the value for the following picture?**

   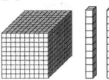

(A)   402

(B)   420

(C)   2200

(D)   4020

Common Core Standard 4.NBT.1 – Numbers & Operations in Base Ten

☐   **What is the value for the following picture?**

(A)   212

(B)   2110

(C)   1110

(D)   4020

Name _____   Date_____

☐   **What is the value for the following picture?**

(A)   513

(B)   1130

(C)   113

(D)   630

Common Core Standard 4.NBT.1 – Numbers & Operations in Base Ten

☐   **What is the correct answer for the value below?**

8 thousands = ☐ tens

(A)   8

(B)   8000

(C)   80

(D)   800

Common Core Standard 4.NBT.1 – Numbers & Operations in Base Ten

☐   **What is the correct answer for the value below?**

4 hundreds = ☐ ones

(A)   4

(B)   400

(C)   40

(D)   4000

Common Core Standard 4.NBT.1 – Numbers & Operations in Base Ten

☐ **What is the correct answer for the value below?**

16 thousands = ☐ hundreds

Ⓐ 160

Ⓑ 1600

Ⓒ 16

Ⓓ 16000

Common Core Standard 4.NBT.1 – Numbers & Operations in Base Ten

☐ **What is the value for the following picture?**

Ⓐ 1210

Ⓑ 2210

Ⓒ 1021

Ⓓ 4210

Common Core Standard 4.NBT.1 – Numbers & Operations in Base Ten

☐ **What is the value for the following picture?**

Ⓐ 534

Ⓑ 840

Ⓒ 1340

Ⓓ 1430

Common Core Standard 4.NBT.1 – Numbers & Operations in Base Ten

☐   **What is the value for the following picture?**

Ⓐ   3130

Ⓑ   1513

Ⓒ   1630

Ⓓ   313

Common Core Standard 4.NBT.1 – Numbers & Operations in Base Ten

☐   **What is the correct answer for the value below?**

20 hundreds = ☐ tens

Ⓐ   200

Ⓑ   20

Ⓒ   2000

Ⓓ   10

Common Core Standard 4.NBT.1 – Numbers & Operations in Base Ten

☐   **What is the correct answer for the value below?**

150 tens = ☐ ones

Ⓐ   15

Ⓑ   150

Ⓒ   1500

Ⓓ   15000

Common Core Standard 4.NBT.1 – Numbers & Operations in Base Ten

☐   **What is the correct answer for the value below?**

9 thousands = ☐ ones

(A)   **9000**

(B)   **900**

(C)   **90**

(D)   **9**

Name _____   Date_____

Common Core Standard 4.NBT.2 – Numbers & Operations in Base Ten

☐   **Which number has a 6 in the ten thousands place and a 4 in the hundreds place?**

(A)   1,636,491

(B)   6,463,941

(C)   1,463,491

(D)   4,636,149

Common Core Standard 4.NBT.2 – Numbers & Operations in Base Ten

☐   **Texas has an area of 267,339 square miles including land covered by water. How is this number of square miles written in words?**

(A)   **Two thousand sixty-seven, three hundred thirty-nine**

(B)   **Two hundred sixty-seven thousand, three thirty-nine**

(C)   **Two million, sixty-seven thousand, three thirty-nine**

(D)   **Two hundred sixty-seven thousand, three hundred thirty-nine**

Common Core Standard 4.NBT.2 – Numbers & Operations in Base Ten

☐   **Which group of numbers is in order from *greatest* to *least*?**

(A)   1,637,537   1,636, 419   1,637,020   1,636,342

(B)   1,637,537   1,637,020   1,636,419   1,636,342

(C)   1,636,342   1,636,419   1,637,020   1,637,537

(D)   1,637,537   1,637,020   1,636,342   1,636,419

Common Core Standard 4.NBT.2 – Numbers & Operations in Base Ten

☐ **Which numeral has a larger digit in the hundreds place than in the tens place?**

(A) 356,281

(B) 1,375,290

(C) 27,192

(D) 6,437

Common Core Standard 4.NBT.2 – Numbers & Operations in Base Ten

☐ **Which group of numbers is in order from *least* to *greatest*?**

(A) 534,874	535,088	535,410	535,743
(B) 535,743	535,410	535,088	534,874
(C) 534,874	535,088	535,743	535,410
(D) 535,743	535,088	535,410	534,874

Common Core Standard 4.NBT.2 – Numbers & Operations in Base Ten

☐ **What is the place value of the 8 in 8,502,734?**

(A) 8 thousand

(B) 8 hundred thousand

(C) 8 million

(D) 8 hundred million

Common Core Standard 4.NBT.2 – Numbers & Operations in Base Ten

[ ]   The fastest growing city in Texas in 1998 was Plano, TX. It grew by fourteen thousand, five hundred people that year. How is this number of people written?

(A)   1,450

(B)   14,500,000

(C)   14,500

(D)   145,500

Common Core Standard 4.NBT.2 – Numbers & Operations in Base Ten

[ ]   Which number has a 9 in the hundreds place?

(A)   469,207

(B)   358,927

(C)   120,493

(D)   893,528

Common Core Standard 4.NBT.2 – Numbers & Operations in Base Ten

[ ]   Which statement is true?

(A)   4,257,138 > 4,257,039

(B)   2,429,236 > 2,429,238

(C)   1,478,533 < 1,478,532

(D)   3,305,131 > 3,305,135

Common Core Standard 4.NBT.2 – Numbers & Operations in Base Ten

☐ What is the place value of the 3 in 538,091?

(A) Hundred thousands

(B) Ten thousands

(C) Thousands

(D) Millions

Common Core Standard 4.NBT.2 – Numbers & Operations in Base Ten

☐ A movie theater kept a record of the number of tickets they sold. In January they sold 5,390 tickets, 5,178 tickets in February, 5,199 tickets in March, and 5,096 tickets in April. Which shows the number of tickets sold in order from *greatest* to *least*?

(A) 5,390   5,096   5,178   5,199

(B) 5,096   5,178   5,199   5,390

(C) 5,390   5,199   5,178   5,096

(D) 5,390   5,178   5,199   5,096

Common Core Standard 4.NBT.2 – Numbers & Operations in Base Ten

☐ It is time for school pictures. The students must line up in order from the tallest to the shortest. April is 48 inches tall, Brad is 56 inches tall, Callie is 50 inches tall, and David is 55 inches tall. In which order should the students line up?

HEIGHT OF STUDENTS

(A) Brad, David, Callie, April

(B) April, Callie, David, Brad

(C) April, Brad, Callie, David

(D) Brad, April, Callie, David

Student	Height in Inches
April	48 in
Brad	56 in
Callie	50 in
David	55 in

Name _____   Date_____

Common Core Standard 4.NBT.2 – Numbers & Operations in Base Ten

☐ Felipe and his brother played a game while they waited for their mother. They each wrote six numbers on a piece of paper, circled one of the numbers, and then exchanged the pieces of paper. Each boy had to make the largest number possible using all of the numbers and place the circled number in the thousands place. What is the largest number Felipe could have made if he used the numbers 9, 4, 6, 3, 7, 1, and the 4 was circled?

(A) 976,431   (C) 134,679

(B) 947,631   (D) 974,631

Common Core Standard 4.NBT.2 – Numbers & Operations in Base Ten

☐ Which number has an 8 in the thousands place and a 6 in the ones place?

(A) 483,566

(B) 528,616

(C) 637,586

(D) 738,862

Common Core Standard 4.NBT.2 – Numbers & Operations in Base Ten

☐ The area of Guinea is 94,964 square miles. How would this area be written in words?

(A) Nine thousand four, nine hundred six and four

(B) Ninety-four, nine hundred sixty-four

(C) Ninety-four thousand, nine hundred sixty-four

(D) Nine hundred four thousand, nine hundred sixty-four

Name _____   Date_____

Common Core Standard 4.NBT.2 – Numbers & Operations in Base Ten

☐   **Which number has a 7 in the ten thousands place?**

(A)   367,201

(B)   2,405,799

(C)   728,458

(D)   970,463

Common Core Standard 4.NBT.2 – Numbers & Operations in Base Ten

☐   **Which statement is true?**

(A) $36 \div 4 > 72 \div 9$

(B) $84 \div 7 > 13 \times 3$

(C) $140 \div 14 = (10 \times 12) \div 12$

(D) $8 \times 15 < 1000 \div 20$

Common Core Standard 4.NBT.2 – Numbers & Operations in Base Ten

☐   **What is the place value of the 8 in 8,030,274?**

(A)   Millions

(B)   Hundred thousands

(C)   Hundred millions

(D)   Ten thousands

Common Core Standard 4.NBT.3 – Numbers & Operations in Base Ten

☐   Derrick counted the number of cars on the school parking lots. There were 116 cars parked at the elementary school and 259 cars parked on the high school parking lot. About how many cars did he count altogether?

Ⓐ   200

Ⓑ   300

Ⓒ   100

Ⓓ   400

Common Core Standard 4.NBT.3 – Numbers & Operations in Base Ten

☐   If a person spends an average of 210 hours per month sleeping, about how many hours does a person sleep in 5 days?

Ⓐ   205 hours

Ⓑ   10 hours

Ⓒ   40 hours

Ⓓ   1,050 hours

Common Core Standard 4.NBT.3 – Numbers & Operations in Base Ten

☐   Marianna spends 48 to 52 minutes a day practicing her ballet dancing. Which is a reasonable total number of minutes she will practice her ballet dancing in 8 days?

Ⓐ   600 min

Ⓑ   400 min

Ⓒ   450 min

Ⓓ   300 min

Common Core Standard 4.NBT.3 – Numbers & Operations in Base Ten

☐ About 781 airplanes have landed at the new airport during its first year. If the same amount of planes land for the next 2 years, about how many planes will have landed since the airport opened?

(A) 1,600

(B) 2,400

(C) 1,562

(D) 1,000

Common Core Standard 4.NBT.3 – Numbers & Operations in Base Ten

☐ Lacey bought a packet of video games on sale. She paid $27 for the games. The suggested retail price of the packet of video games is from $49 to $55. Which could be the amount Lacey saved by buying the games on sale rather than paying the suggested retail price?

(A) $5

(B) $40

(C) $10

(D) $20

Common Core Standard 4.NBT.3 – Numbers & Operations in Base Ten

☐ Kathryn's score on a video game was 3,752. What is her score rounded to the nearest hundred?

(A) 3,700

(B) 3,750

(C) 3,800

(D) 4,000

Common Core Standard 4.NBT.3 – Numbers & Operations in Base Ten

☐   Marcus wanted to buy a shirt that costs $14.79, a pair of slacks that costs $29.50, and some socks that cost $6.99. *About* how much will he spend for the three items?

(A) $45

(B) $50

(C) $52

(D) $47

Common Core Standard 4.NBT.3 – Numbers & Operations in Base Ten

☐   Kirk, Jamie, and Kerry went to lunch together last Saturday. Kirk's bill was $5.25, Jamie's bill was $5.49, and Kerry's lunch cost $4.95. About how much did they spend altogether for lunch?

(A) $15

(B) $20

(C) $17

(D) $16

Common Core Standard 4.NBT.3 – Numbers & Operations in Base Ten

☐   It is 797 miles from Dallas to Denver, Colorado. If Paul's father drives 60 miles per hour, about how long will it take his family to make the trip?

(A) 737 hours

(B) 2 hours

(C) 857 hours

(D) 13 hours

Name _____   Date_____

Common Core Standard 4.NBT.3 – Numbers & Operations in Base Ten

[ ]   Mr. Simmons drives 29 to 33 miles a day going from his house to his job. Which is a reasonable total number of miles he will drive in 11 days?

(A)   330 mi

(B)   250 mi

(C)   420 mi

(D)   370 mi

Common Core Standard 4.NBT.3 – Numbers & Operations in Base Ten

[ ]   The fourth grade classes are selling cookies to raise money for new gym equipment. If a class has 22 students and they each bring 2 dozen cookies, about how many cookies will a class sell?

(A)   46 cookies

(B)   100 cookies

(C)   400 cookies

(D)   600 cookies

Common Core Standard 4.NBT.3 – Numbers & Operations in Base Ten

[ ]   Mr. Woods bought a big screen television from a friend who was moving to England. The television would have cost from $1250 to $1500 if he had bought it new. If Mr. Woods paid his friend $520 for the television, which could be the approximate amount he saved by buying it from his friend rather than buying a new television?

(A) $1100

(B) $500

(C) $900

(D) $700

Name _____   Date_____

Common Core Standard 4.NBT.3 – Numbers & Operations in Base Ten

☐   Benjamin's family traveled 1,559 miles on their vacation. What is their mileage rounded to the nearest hundred?

(A)   2,000 mi

(B)   1,560 mi

(C)   1,500 mi

(D)   1,600 mi

Common Core Standard 4.NBT.3 – Numbers & Operations in Base Ten

☐   Darius only brought $5 for lunch. Which of the items can he purchase and not spend more than $5?

(A)   Bologna sandwich and a cola

(B)   Chicken sandwich and soup

(C)   Soup and tea

(D)   BLT sandwich and a cola

THE CAFE	
Soup	$5.99
Sandwiches	
Chicken	$4.99
BLT	$4.50
Bologna	$2.90
Drinks	
Cola	$1.15
Tea	$0.95

Common Core Standard 4.NBT.3 – Numbers & Operations in Base Ten

☐   Dante added 1,468 and 3,704. Which could be an estimate of the total?

(A)   6,000

(B)   5,200

(C)   5,100

(D)   3,000

Name _____ Date_____

Common Core Standard 4.NBT.4 – Numbers & Operations in Base Ten

☐ The Christmas parade is Saturday. Mr. Black believes that many people will buy cookies from his bakery while at the parade. In order to get ready for Saturday his bakery baked 456 cookies on Wednesday. On Thursday he baked 321 cookies, and on Friday he baked 478 cookies. How many cookies did he bake on those 3 days?

(A) 1,145 cookies

(B) 1,355 cookies

(C) 1,255 cookies

(D) 1,265 cookies

Common Core Standard 4.NBT.4 – Numbers & Operations in Base Ten

☐ A new building in Betina's hometown is 1,207 feet tall. The building next to it is 897 feet tall. If the buildings were stacked on top of each other, how tall would they be altogether?

(A) 1,094 ft

(B) 2,104 ft

(C) 2,004 ft

(D) 1,104 ft

Common Core Standard 4.NBT.4 – Numbers & Operations in Base Ten

☐ Mrs. Black bought a new dining room suite. The table cost $1,042, the chairs were $599, and the china cabinet was $755. How much did she spend altogether, not including tax?

(A) $2,386

(B) $1,386

(C) $2,496

(D) $2,396

Name _____   Date_____

Common Core Standard 4.NBT.4 – Numbers & Operations in Base Ten

☐   Carter Elementary spent $2,086 on new books for the library. The librarian spent $95 on additional shelves for the new books. How much was spent altogether?

(A) $2,071

(B) $2,081

(C) $2,181

(D) $1,991

Common Core Standard 4.NBT.4 – Numbers & Operations in Base Ten

☐   A county fair had 2,852 people in attendance on Friday, 4,199 people on Saturday, and 3,005 people on Sunday. What was the total number of people who attended the fair on those 3 days?

(A) 9,946

(B) 10,056

(C) 10,066

(D) 10,156

Common Core Standard 4.NBT.4 – Numbers & Operations in Base Ten

☐   A city had 115 entries in the Christmas parade, 68 entries in the Easter parade, and 101 entries in the Fourth of July parade. What was the total number of entries in the 3 parades?

Record your answer and fill in the bubbles on your answer document. Be sure to use the correct place value.

⓪	⓪	⓪	
①	①	①	
②	②	②	
③	③	③	
④	④	④	
⑤	⑤	⑤	
⑥	⑥	⑥	
⑦	⑦	⑦	
⑧	⑧	⑧	
⑨	⑨	⑨	

Name _____ Date_____

Common Core Standard 4.NBT.4 – Numbers & Operations in Base Ten

☐ What is the difference between the distance of 1,700 miles that Beverly's family traveled on their vacation and the distance of 99 miles that Cameron's family traveled last weekend?

(A) 1,799 miles

(B) 1,601 miles

(C) 1,611 miles

(D) 1,711 miles

Common Core Standard 4.NBT.4 – Numbers & Operations in Base Ten

☐ Carley's class collected 4,954 cans last year. If they collected 1,976 cans before January, how many cans were collected after January?

(A) 3,978

(B) 6,930

(C) 2,978

(D) 3,088

Common Core Standard 4.NBT.4 – Numbers & Operations in Base Ten

☐ Adela has saved $192 to buy school clothes for her sister and herself. When she and her sister went shopping, they found that they needed $351, including tax, to buy the clothes they had chosen. How much more money does Adela need to buy the school clothes?

(A) $159

(B) $543

(C) $269

(D) $169

Common Core Standard 4.NBT.4 – Numbers & Operations in Base Ten

☐ Jonesville has a population of 4,257,388 people. Lake City has a population of 7,125,210 people. How much larger is Lake City than Jonesville?

(A) 2,867,822

(B) 3,132,178

(C) 3,978,932

(D) 2,868,822

Common Core Standard 4.NBT.4 – Numbers & Operations in Base Ten

☐ A grocery store sold 1,328 pounds of poultry during Thanksgiving. This was 449 pounds more than they sold last year. How many pounds of poultry did they sell last year?

(A) 889 lbs

(B) 879 lbs

(C) 1,777 lbs

(D) 989 lbs

Common Core Standard 4.NBT.4 – Numbers & Operations in Base Ten

☐ The Crandle family went to Canada on their vacation. They spent part of the time traveling in their car and the rest of the time traveling in an airplane. They traveled 2,175 miles in their car. What additional information is needed to find out how many miles were traveled in an airplane?

(A) No additional information is needed.

(B) The number of days they were gone

(C) The total number of miles they traveled

(D) The number of people who went on the vacation

Name _____   Date_____

☐   Tameka made a bead picture for her mother. She used 138 beads for the sky, 59 beads for the grass, and 92 beads for the flowers. The bag of beads contained 750 beads before she began her picture. How many beads were left in the package after she finished her picture?

Record your answer and fill in the bubbles on your answer document. Be sure to use the correct place value.

⓪	⓪	⓪	
①	①	①	
②	②	②	
③	③	③	
④	④	④	
⑤	⑤	⑤	
⑥	⑥	⑥	
⑦	⑦	⑦	
⑧	⑧	⑧	
⑨	⑨	⑨	

☐   Hope's older sister took her scooter in for repairs. The mechanic told her it would cost $48 for parts, $25 for paint, and $28 for new chrome, plus the labor charges. What other information is needed to find the total cost of the repairs to the scooter?

(A)   The color of the scooter

(B)   The age of the scooter

(C)   The length of time to repair the scooter

(D)   The charges for labor

☐   Derrick had 632 baseball cards. He wanted to sell some of them so he could buy 50 action figures. He sold 238 of the baseball cards to a hobby store. Which shows the number of baseball cards Derrick did *not* sell?

(A)   238 + 50

(B)   632 – 238

(C)   632 – 238 + 50

(D)   632 ÷ 238

Common Core Standard 4.NBT.5 – Numbers & Operations in Base Ten

☐ There are 20 school days in one month. Adela brought 27 pencils for each of her fourth grade classmates 13 times during the month. How many pencils did Adela bring to school in 1 month?

Ⓐ 40

Ⓑ 540

Ⓒ 7,020

Ⓓ 351

Common Core Standard 4.NBT.5 – Numbers & Operations in Base Ten

☐ Andrew saves his allowance. He receives $15 a week for doing chores for his family. How much money will he save in 9 weeks?

Ⓐ $24

Ⓑ $135

Ⓒ $95

Ⓓ $145

Common Core Standard 4.NBT.5 – Numbers & Operations in Base Ten

☐ Kelly's mother baked 25 pans of cookies to sell at a school carnival. There were 36 cookies on each pan. How many cookies did she bake for the carnival?

Ⓐ 900

Ⓑ 71

Ⓒ 800

Ⓓ 899

Common Core Standard 4.NBT.5 – Numbers & Operations in Base Ten

☐ The chart gives the cost for a year's subscription for 4 different magazines. How much will a 15 year subscription to "Sports Legends" cost?

(A) $60

(B) $51

(C) $440

(D) $540

Magazine	Cost of Subscription
Greatest Adventures	$18
International Traveler	$25
Outdoor Cooking	$30
Sports Legends	$36

Common Core Standard 4.NBT.5 – Numbers & Operations in Base Ten

☐ What information is needed to solve the following problem?

> Miranda slept 7 hours every night when she stayed with her grandparents. How many hours did she sleep altogether?

(A) The number of people in Miranda's family

(B) The age of Miranda

(C) The number of days Miranda spent at her grandparents

(D) No more information is needed.

Common Core Standard 4.NBT.5 – Numbers & Operations in Base Ten

☐ Amanda, Brooke, and Bennett ordered 2 large sausage pizzas and 3 large cheese pizzas for a party. The large pizzas each cost $9. Which method could be used to find the total cost of the order?

(A) Add $9 to the sum of 2 and 3

(B) Add 2 and 3, multiply by $9

(C) Subtract 3 from $9, multiply by 2

(D) Multiply 2 and 3, add $9

Common Core Standard 4.NBT.5 – Numbers & Operations in Base Ten

☐ Spencer earns $15 for caring for cats during weekends. Jasmine earns $5.35 for each dog she takes care of during a weekend. How much more would Jasmine earn than Spencer if she cared for 3 pets during a weekend?

(A) $9.65

(B) $16.05

(C) $31.05

(D) $1.05

Common Core Standard 4.NBT.5 – Numbers & Operations in Base Ten

☐ Drew has been running for 3 months trying to earn a place on the track team. He runs 4 miles each day after school and rests on the weekends. Which method could be used to find the total number of miles he will run in 15 days?

(A) Add 3 and 4, multiply by 15

(B) Multiply 15 by 4

(C) Subtract 3 from 4, multiply by 15

(D) Add 3, 4, and 15

Common Core Standard 4.NBT.5 – Numbers & Operations in Base Ten

☐ It is said that 1 human year is equal to 7 years for a dog. Christian's dog had puppies on his 9th birthday. Which number sentence shows how to find how old the puppies will be in dog years when Christian is 14 years old?

(A) $9 \times (14 - 7) = 63$

(B) $9 \times (1 + 7) = 72$

(C) $(14 - 9) \times 7 = 35$

(D) $14 \times (14 - 7) = 98$

Name _____   Date_____

Common Core Standard 4.NBT.5 – Numbers & Operations in Base Ten

☐   Each fourth grade class at Turner Intermediate has 22 students. Each student was given 2 pencils the first day of school. If there are 15 fourth grade classes, how many pencils were given to the fourth grade students?

Record your answer and fill in the bubbles on your answer document. Be sure to use the correct place value.

⓪	⓪	⓪	
①	①	①	
②	②	②	
③	③	③	
④	④	④	
⑤	⑤	⑤	
⑥	⑥	⑥	
⑦	⑦	⑦	
⑧	⑧	⑧	
⑨	⑨	⑨	

Common Core Standard 4.NBT.5 – Numbers & Operations in Base Ten

☐   Reid has been collecting baseball cards for 5 years. He has 37 boxes with 75 cards in each box. How many baseball cards has Reid collected?

(A)   375

(B)   2,775

(C)   185

(D)   560

Common Core Standard 4.NBT.5 – Numbers & Operations in Base Ten

☐   Robin's mother made 7 flower beds in the front yard. She wants to plant 23 bushes in each bed. How many bushes will she plant in the front yard?

Record your answer and fill in the bubbles on your answer document. Be sure to use the correct place value.

⓪	⓪	⓪	
①	①	①	
②	②	②	
③	③	③	
④	④	④	
⑤	⑤	⑤	
⑥	⑥	⑥	
⑦	⑦	⑦	
⑧	⑧	⑧	
⑨	⑨	⑨	

Name _____   Date_____

Common Core Standard 4.NBT.5 – Numbers & Operations in Base Ten

☐   Dominique has a paper route. A subscription for the newspaper costs $27 per month. If Dominique has 39 customers, what is the total amount of money that he earns in a month?

Ⓐ $1,056

Ⓑ $793

Ⓒ $1,033

Ⓓ $1,053

Common Core Standard 4.NBT.5 – Numbers & Operations in Base Ten

☐   The chart shows the sales in dollars that Ben's Seafood Company made in a month. How much money will the company make in shrimp sales in 36 months?

Ⓐ $3,564

Ⓑ $2,808

Ⓒ $114

Ⓓ $2,828

Kind of Seafood	Sales in Dollars
Lobster	$99
Oyster	$104
Shrimp	$78
Crab	$59

Common Core Standard 4.NBT.5 – Numbers & Operations in Base Ten

☐   What information is needed to solve the following problem?

The fourth grade classes had a raffle for a skateboard. Each of the students were given 25 tickets to sell. How many tickets were sold?

Ⓐ   The number of students in the fourth grade classes

Ⓑ   The price of each raffle ticket

Ⓒ   The name of the school

Ⓓ   No more information is needed.

Name _____   Date_____

Common Core Standard 4.NBT.6 – Numbers & Operations in Base Ten

☐   **If 6 times a number is 30, which expression could be used to find the number?**

(A)   30 + 6

(B)   30 − 6

(C)   30 × 6

(D)   30 ÷ 6

Common Core Standard 4.NBT.6 – Numbers & Operations in Base Ten

☐   **Which number sentence is in the same family of facts as 21 ÷ 7 = 3?**

(A)   21 − 7 = 14

(B)   7 × 3 = 21

(C)   7 + 3 = 10

(D)   21 × 7 = 147

Common Core Standard 4.NBT.6 – Numbers & Operations in Base Ten

☐   **One of the number sentences in the box does not belong with the others. Which number sentence is it?**

(A)   9 × 4 = 36

(B)   36 ÷ 4 = 9

(C)   9 + 4 = 13

(D)   36 ÷ 9 = 4

| 9 × 4 = 36 |
| 9 + 4 = 13 |
| 36 ÷ 4 = 9 |
| 36 ÷ 9 = 4 |

Common Core Standard 4.NBT.6 – Numbers & Operations in Base Ten

☐   **Which number sentence is in the same family of facts as 4 × 5 = 20?**

(A)   4 + 5 = 9

(B)   20 ÷ 5 = 4

(C)   10 × 2 = 20

(D)   20 − 5 = 15

Common Core Standard 4.NBT.6 – Numbers & Operations in Base Ten

☐   **Isaac works in the school store. He wants to place 44 mini erasers into 11 bags. Which pair of related facts would show how many erasers he can place in each bag and be correct?**

(A)   11 + 4 = 15;   15 − 11 = 4

(B)   4 × 2 = 8;   8 ÷ 2 = 4

(C)   44 ÷ 11 = 4;   11 × 4 = 44

(D)   44 − 11 = 33;   33 + 11 = 44

Common Core Standard 4.NBT.6 – Numbers & Operations in Base Ten

☐   **If 60 ÷ 12 = ☐ , then 60 ÷ ☐ = 12. Which numeral would fit in both number sentences?**

(A)   5

(B)   1

(C)   72

(D)   48

Common Core Standard 4.NBT.6 – Numbers & Operations in Base Ten

☐ **Which number sentence should not have a 6 in the box?**

(A) $24 \div 4 = \square$

(B) $36 \div \square = 6$

(C) $48 \div \square = 6$

(D) $54 \div 9 = \square$

Common Core Standard 4.NBT.6 – Numbers & Operations in Base Ten

☐ **If 8 times a number is 48, which expression could be used to find the number?**

(A) 8×48

(B) $48 \div 8$

(C) $8 + 48$

(D) $48 - 8$

Common Core Standard 4.NBT.6 – Numbers & Operations in Base Ten

☐ **Which number sentence is in the same family of facts as $56 \div 8 = 7$?**

(A) $8 + 7 = 15$

(B) $56 - 8 = 48$

(C) $56 \times 7 = 392$

(D) $8 \times 7 = 56$

Common Core Standard 4.NBT.6 – Numbers & Operations in Base Ten

☐ One of the number sentences in the box does not belong with the others. Which number sentence does not belong?

(A) 45 - 5 = 40

(B) 9 × 5 = 45

(C) 45 ÷ 5 = 9

(D) 45 ÷ 9 = 5

```
45 ÷ 9 = 5

9 × 5 = 45

45 – 5 = 40

45 ÷ 5 = 9
```

Common Core Standard 4.NBT.6 – Numbers & Operations in Base Ten

☐ Which number sentence is in the same family of facts as 2 × 12 = 24?

(A) 12 – 2 = 10

(B) 24 × 2 = 48

(C) 24 ÷ 12 = 2

(D) 24 + 12 = 36

Common Core Standard 4.NBT.6 – Numbers & Operations in Base Ten

☐ Hailey bought 6 containers for her CDs. She has 42 CDs that she needs to store. Which pair of related facts would show how many CDs she can place in each container and be correct?

(A) 42 × 6 = 252;   252 ÷ 6 = 42

(B) 42 – 7 = 35;   7 + 35 = 42

(C) 42 + 6 = 48;   42 – 6 = 36

(D) 42 ÷ 6 = 7;   6 × 7 = 42

Common Core Standard 4.NBT.6 – Numbers & Operations in Base Ten

☐   If $54 \div 9 =$ ☐ , then $54 \div$ ☐ $= 9$. Which numeral would be correct in both number sentences?

(A)   7

(B)   486

(C)   6

(D)   63

Common Core Standard 4.NBT.6 – Numbers & Operations in Base Ten

☐   Which number sentence should not have a 9 in the box?

(A) $56 \div$ ☐ $= 8$

(B) $36 \div 4 =$ ☐

(C) $27 \div$ ☐ $= 3$

(D) $54 \div 6 =$ ☐

Common Core Standard 4.NBT.6 – Numbers & Operations in Base Ten

☐   If 12 times a number is 36, which expression could be used to find the number?

(A) 36×12

(B) $36 + 12$

(C) $36 \div 12$

(D) $36 - 12$

Common Core Standard 4.NBT.6 – Numbers & Operations in Base Ten

☐ **Which number sentence is in the same family of facts as 28 ÷ 4 = 7?**

Ⓐ $28 \times 7 = 196$

Ⓑ $28 - 7 = 21$

Ⓒ $4 \times 7 = 28$

Ⓓ $4 + 7 = 11$

Common Core Standard 4.NBT.6 – Numbers & Operations in Base Ten

☐ **One of the number sentences in the box does not belong with the others. Which number sentence is it?**

Ⓐ $8 \times 9 = 72$

Ⓑ $72 + 9 = 81$

Ⓒ $72 \div 9 = 8$

Ⓓ $9 \times 8 = 72$

> $8 \times 9 = 72$
>
> $72 \div 9 = 8$
>
> $72 + 9 = 81$
>
> $9 \times 8 = 72$

Common Core Standard 4.NBT.6 – Numbers & Operations in Base Ten

☐ **Which number sentence is in the same family of facts as 8 × 4 = 32?**

Ⓐ $32 - 4 = 28$

Ⓑ $32 \times 8 = 256$

Ⓒ $8 + 4 = 12$

Ⓓ $32 \div 8 = 4$

Common Core Standard 4.NF.1 – Numbers & Operations - Fractions

[   ]   **Look at the shaded parts of the circles. Which statement shows this fraction model?**

(A) $\dfrac{2}{3} > \dfrac{2}{6}$

(B) $\dfrac{1}{3} = \dfrac{2}{6}$

(C) $\dfrac{1}{4} < \dfrac{3}{8}$

(D) $\dfrac{1}{3} > \dfrac{4}{6}$

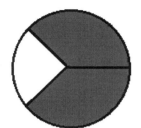
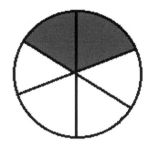

Common Core Standard 4.NF.1 – Numbers & Operations - Fractions

[   ]   **Which of the models is equivalent to $\dfrac{1}{2}$?**

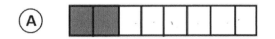

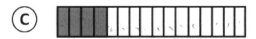

Common Core Standard 4.NF.1 – Numbers & Operations - Fractions

[   ]   **Which model does *not* show an equivalent fraction for $\dfrac{1}{4}$?**

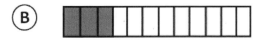

Common Core Standard 4.NF.1 – Numbers & Operations - Fractions

☐   The figures are shaded to show equivalent fractions. Which fraction is equivalent to $\frac{2}{8}$?

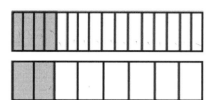

Ⓐ $\frac{1}{4}$ Ⓒ $\frac{4}{8}$

Ⓑ $\frac{2}{4}$ Ⓓ $\frac{12}{16}$

Common Core Standard 4.NF.1 – Numbers & Operations - Fractions

☐   Which of the models is equivalent to $\frac{2}{3}$?

Ⓐ    Ⓒ

Ⓑ 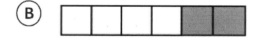   Ⓓ

Common Core Standard 4.NF.1 – Numbers & Operations - Fractions

☐   Which model does *not* show an equivalent fraction for $\frac{2}{3}$?

Ⓐ    Ⓒ

Ⓑ 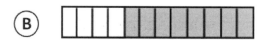   Ⓓ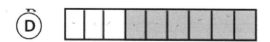

Name _____   Date_____

Common Core Standard 4.NF.1 – Numbers & Operations – Fractions

☐   **Which pair of figures shows congruent fractions?**

Ⓐ 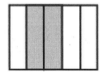   Ⓒ

Ⓑ   Ⓓ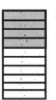

Common Core Standard 4.NF.1 – Numbers & Operations - Fractions

☐   **The figures are shaded to show equivalent fractions. Which fraction is equivalent to $\frac{3}{5}$?**

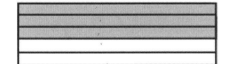   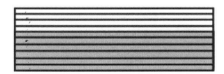

Ⓐ $\frac{4}{6}$ Ⓒ $\frac{6}{4}$

Ⓑ $\frac{4}{10}$ Ⓓ $\frac{6}{10}$

Common Core Standard 4.NF.1 – Numbers & Operations - Fractions

☐   **Which of the models is equivalent to $\frac{3}{5}$?**

Ⓐ    Ⓒ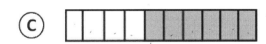

Ⓑ    Ⓓ

Common Core Standard 4.NF.1 – Numbers & Operations - Fractions

☐ **Which model does *not* show an equivalent fraction for $\frac{1}{6}$?**

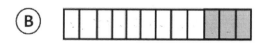

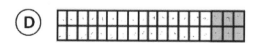

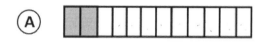

Common Core Standard 4.NF.1 – Numbers & Operations - Fractions

☐ **Look at the shaded parts of the models. Which models show $\frac{2}{10}$ = $\frac{1}{5}$?**

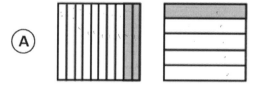

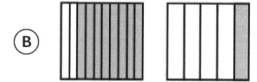

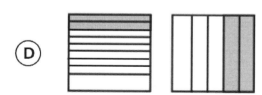

Common Core Standard 4.NF.1 – Numbers & Operations – Fractions

☐ **Which pair of figures shows congruent fractions?**

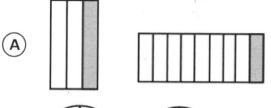

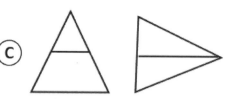

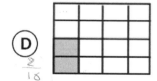

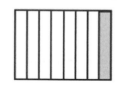

Common Core Standard 4.NF.1 – Numbers & Operations - Fractions

☐   The figures are shaded to show equivalent fractions. Which fraction is equivalent to $\frac{6}{7}$?

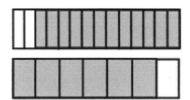

Ⓐ $\frac{6}{14}$ Ⓒ $\frac{6}{12}$

Ⓑ $\frac{12}{14}$ Ⓓ $\frac{1}{7}$

Common Core Standard 4.NF.1 – Numbers & Operations – Fractions

☐   Look at the model. Which fraction is shown by the model?

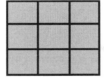 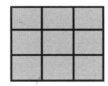 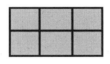

Ⓐ $\frac{24}{18}$ Ⓒ $\frac{24}{9}$

Ⓑ $\frac{9}{24}$ Ⓓ $\frac{6}{18}$

Common Core Standard 4.NF.1 – Numbers & Operations - Fractions

☐   Which fraction does the model below represent?

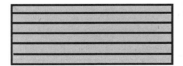 

Ⓐ $1\frac{2}{8}$ Ⓒ $\frac{2}{6}$

Ⓑ $1\frac{1}{3}$ Ⓓ $\frac{6}{2}$

Name _____   Date_____

Common Core Standard 4.NF.2 – Numbers & Operations - Fractions

 Look at the shaded parts of the models. Which models show $\frac{1}{4} < \frac{3}{9}$?

 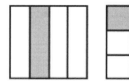

Common Core Standard 4.NF.2 – Numbers & Operations – Fractions

 **Which statement is true?**

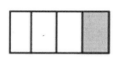 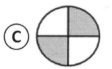

Ⓐ   =   **Ⓒ**   =

Ⓑ   =   **Ⓓ**   =

Common Core Standard 4.NF.2 – Numbers & Operations - Fractions

Look at the shaded parts of the figures. Which statement shows the fraction model?

Ⓐ $\frac{9}{12} = \frac{1}{9}$

Ⓑ $\frac{9}{18} > \frac{1}{2}$

Ⓒ $\frac{9}{18} = \frac{1}{2}$

Ⓓ $\frac{9}{18} < \frac{1}{4}$

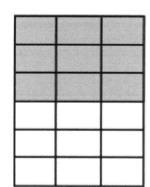 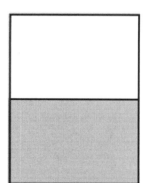

Common Core Standard 4.NF.2 – Numbers & Operations - Fractions

□ If = $\frac{1}{4}$, = $\frac{1}{2}$, = $\frac{1}{8}$, and ☆ = $\frac{1}{3}$, which of the
following would be in the correct order from *greatest* to *least*?

(A) ☆ ○ □ △

(B) ○ △ □ ☆

(C) △ ☆ ○ □

(D) △ ○ ☆ □

Common Core Standard 4.NF.2 – Numbers & Operations - Fractions

□ Which of the following fractions would come next in the series if a
fraction were used instead of the model?

(A) $\frac{5}{5}$

(B) $\frac{4}{5}$

(C) $\frac{1}{2}$

(D) $\frac{1}{5}$

Common Core Standard 4.NF.2 – Numbers & Operations - Fractions

□ Look at the shaded figures in each row in the box. Which two rows
are equivalent fractions based on the shaded figures?

(A) Rows 1 and 2

(B) Rows 2 and 3

(C) Rows 3 and 4

(D) Rows 2 and 4

Common Core Standard 4.NF.2 – Numbers & Operations - Fractions

☐   **Which statement is true?**

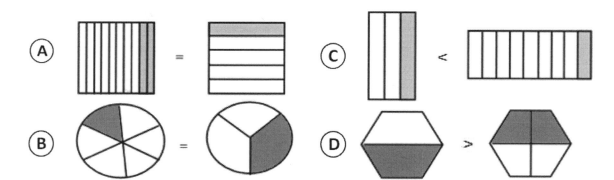

Common Core Standard 4.NF.2 – Numbers & Operations - Fractions

☐   **Molly's grandmother makes delicious cornbread. Her recipe uses $\frac{3}{4}$ cup of cornmeal, $\frac{1}{2}$ cup of flour, and $\frac{2}{3}$ cup of milk. Which list of fractions shows the ingredients Molly's grandmother uses in order from least to greatest?**

Ⓐ $\frac{1}{2}, \frac{2}{3}, \frac{3}{4}$ Ⓒ $\frac{2}{3}, \frac{3}{4}, \frac{1}{2}$

Ⓑ $\frac{3}{4}, \frac{1}{2}, \frac{2}{3}$ Ⓓ $\frac{3}{4}, \frac{2}{3}, \frac{1}{2}$

Common Core Standard 4.NF.2 – Numbers & Operations - Fractions

☐   **Madison and Trent are having a discussion about fractions. Trent believes $\frac{2}{10}$ is less than $\frac{1}{3}$. Which models can he use to prove his belief is true?**

Ⓐ   1 and 4

Ⓑ   1 and 3

Ⓒ   3 and 4

Ⓓ   2 and 4

1

2

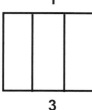

3

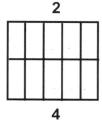

4

Common Core Standard 4.NF.2 – Numbers & Operations - Fractions

☐ Mariah, Jamie, and Destiny each bought a candy bar. Mariah ate $\frac{1}{2}$ of her candy bar. Jamie ate $\frac{1}{3}$ of hers, and Destiny ate $\frac{5}{8}$ of her candy bar. Which shows who has eaten the candy bars in order from the greatest to the least?

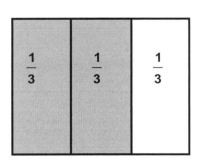

(A) Destiny, Jamie, Mariah   (C) Mariah, Destiny, Jamie

(B) Destiny, Mariah, Jamie   (D) Jamie, Mariah, Destiny

Common Core Standard 4.NF.2 – Numbers & Operations - Fractions

☐ An art teacher is checking the supply of tempera paint. She has $\frac{3}{4}$ of a gallon of orange paint, $\frac{1}{2}$ of a gallon of yellow paint, and $\frac{1}{8}$ of a gallon of white paint. If she places the containers in order from the least amount of paint to the greatest amount of paint, which of the following would be correct?

(A) Orange, yellow, white   (C) White, orange, yellow

(B) Yellow, white, orange   (D) White, yellow, orange

Common Core Standard 4.NF.2 – Numbers & Operations - Fractions

☐ The models are shaded to show that _____

(A) $\frac{2}{3} < \frac{1}{6}$

(B) $\frac{1}{3} = \frac{1}{6}$

(C) $\frac{5}{6} > \frac{2}{3}$

(D) $\frac{2}{3} > \frac{5}{6}$

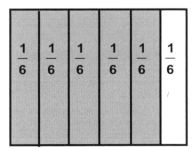

Common Core Standard 4.NF.2 – Numbers & Operations - Fractions

☐ Hope bought $\frac{3}{6}$ of a pound of chocolate candy. Jennifer bought $\frac{2}{12}$ of a pound of the same kind of candy. Which statement can be used to show a comparison of Hope and Jennifer's candy purchases?

(A) $\frac{3}{6}$ is equal to $\frac{2}{12}$

(C) $\frac{1}{8}$ is less than $\frac{3}{4}$

(B) $\frac{3}{6}$ is greater than $\frac{2}{12}$

(D) $\frac{3}{6}$ is less than

Common Core Standard 4.NF.2 – Numbers & Operations - Fractions

☐ A city's basketball teams have both boys and girls on each team. The Dribblers are made up of $\frac{6}{10}$ girls, and the Racers are made up of $\frac{5}{12}$ girls. Which statement is a correct comparison of the number of girls on each team?

(A) $\frac{6}{10} > \frac{5}{12}$ (C) $\frac{5}{12} = \frac{6}{10}$

(B) $\frac{6}{10} < \frac{5}{12}$ (D) $\frac{6}{12} = \frac{5}{10}$

Dribblers

Racers

Common Core Standard 4.NF.2 – Numbers & Operations - Fractions

☐ Look at the figures. Which shows the shaded portions of the figures in order from least to greatest?

(A) $\frac{5}{8}, \frac{3}{8}, \frac{3}{4}$

(B) $\frac{3}{8}, \frac{5}{8}, \frac{3}{4}$

(C) $\frac{3}{4}, \frac{3}{8}, \frac{5}{8}$

(D) $\frac{3}{8}, \frac{3}{4}, \frac{5}{8}$

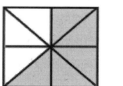
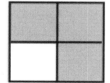
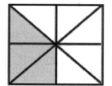

Common Core Standard 4.NF.3 – Numbers & Operations – Fractions

☐   **The 2 shapes are shaded to show that _____**

(A) $\frac{7}{8} > \frac{3}{4}$

(B) $\frac{1}{4} < \frac{1}{8}$

| $\frac{1}{8}$ | $\frac{1}{8}$ | $\frac{1}{8}$ | $\frac{1}{8}$ | $\frac{1}{8}$ | $\frac{1}{8}$ | $\frac{1}{8}$ | $\frac{1}{8}$ |

(C) $\frac{3}{4} = \frac{7}{8}$

(D) $\frac{1}{8} > \frac{1}{4}$

| $\frac{1}{4}$ | $\frac{1}{4}$ | $\frac{1}{4}$ | $\frac{1}{4}$ |

Common Core Standard 4.NF.3 – Numbers & Operations – Fractions

☐   **Which statement can be used to show a comparison of $\frac{6}{8}$ and $\frac{5}{15}$?**

(A) $\frac{5}{15}$ is greater than $\frac{6}{8}$

(C) $\frac{5}{15}$ is equal to $\frac{6}{8}$

(B) $\frac{6}{8}$ is less than $\frac{5}{15}$

(D) $\frac{6}{8}$ is greater than $\frac{5}{15}$

Common Core Standard 4.NF.3 – Numbers & Operations – Fractions

☐   **Compare the fraction models. Which statement is the same as the model?**

   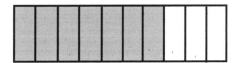

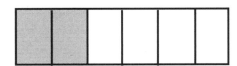

(A) $\frac{2}{5} = \frac{7}{10} = \frac{2}{6}$

(C) $\frac{2}{5} > \frac{7}{10} > \frac{2}{6}$

(B) $\frac{7}{10} > \frac{2}{5} > \frac{2}{6}$

(D) $\frac{1}{4} < \frac{2}{10} < \frac{9}{9}$

Name _____   Date_____

Common Core Standard 4.NF.3 – Numbers & Operations – Fractions

 Which of the following best represents $\frac{10}{12} > \frac{9}{12}$ **?**

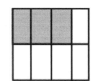 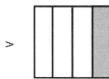 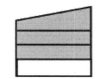 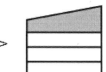

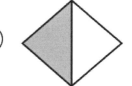 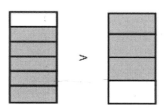

Common Core Standard 4.NF.3 – Numbers & Operations – Fractions

Which models are shaded to show that

(A) $\frac{1}{2} < \frac{1}{5}$

(B) $\frac{3}{5} > \frac{1}{2}$

(C) $\frac{1}{2} = \frac{3}{5}$

(D) $\frac{2}{5} > \frac{1}{2}$

 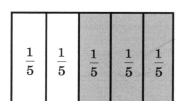

Common Core Standard 4.NF.3 – Numbers & Operations – Fractions

Which statement can be used to show a comparison of $\frac{3}{12}$ **and** $\frac{2}{8}$ **?**

(A) $\frac{3}{12}$ is greater than $\frac{2}{8}$ 　　　(C) $\frac{2}{8}$ is equal to $\frac{3}{12}$

(B) $\frac{2}{8}$ is less than $\frac{3}{12}$ 　　　(D) $\frac{3}{12}$ is less than $\frac{2}{8}$

Name _____   **Date** _____

Common Core Standard 4.NF.3 – Numbers & Operations – Fractions

[ ] **Look at the models. Which statement compares the models correctly?**

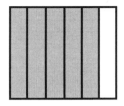 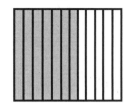 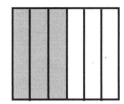

(A) $\frac{3}{6}$ > $\frac{5}{6}$ < $\frac{7}{12}$

(C) $\frac{5}{6}$ > $\frac{7}{12}$ = $\frac{3}{6}$

(B) $\frac{3}{6}$ < $\frac{5}{6}$ < $\frac{7}{12}$

(D) $\frac{7}{12}$ > $\frac{3}{6}$ < $\frac{5}{6}$

Common Core Standard 4.NF.3 – Numbers & Operations – Fractions

[ ] **Look at the shaded parts of the figures. Which figures show $\frac{3}{8}$ > $\frac{1}{4}$?**

(A)

(C)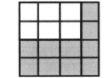

(B)

(D)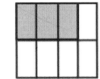

Common Core Standard 4.NF.3 – Numbers & Operations – Fractions

[ ] **Which statement is true?**

(A)

(C)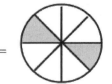

(B)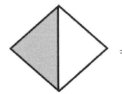

(D)

Common Core Standard 4.NF.3 – Numbers & Operations – Fractions

 **Look at the shaded parts of the circles. Which statement shows the fraction model?**

(A) $\dfrac{1}{3} = \dfrac{5}{8}$

(B) $\dfrac{3}{4} > \dfrac{5}{8}$

(C) $\dfrac{3}{4} = \dfrac{3}{8}$

(D) $\dfrac{1}{4} > \dfrac{5}{8}$

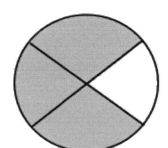
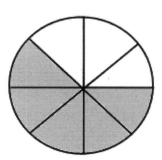

Common Core Standard 4.NF.4 – Numbers & Operations – Fractions

☐ Jose had 6 baseball cards. He gave his friend Sean ½ of his cards. How many cards did Sean get?

(A) $^{1}/_{12}$ cards   (C) 3 cards

(B) 6.2 cards   (D) $^{7}/_{2}$ cards

Common Core Standard 4.NF.4 – Numbers & Operations – Fractions

☐ Select the correct answer for the following statement:

$$5 \times \,^{6}/_{2} \,=$$

(A) 15

(B) $^{6}/_{10}$

(C) $^{11}/_{12}$

(D) $^{3}/_{5}$

Common Core Standard 4.NF.4 – Numbers & Operations – Fractions

☐ Mary drank 6 glasses of water. Each glass was $^{1}/_{3}$ of a cup full when she drank it. How many cups did Mary drink?

(A) $^{7}/_{3}$ cups   (C) 2.1 cups

(B) 2 cups   (D) $^{1}/_{8}$ cups

Common Core Standard 4.NF.4 – Numbers & Operations – Fractions

☐   Select the correct answer for the following statement:

$$3 \times \frac{4}{3} =$$

Ⓐ $\frac{4}{9}$

Ⓑ $\frac{7}{3}$

Ⓒ $\frac{1}{2}$

Ⓓ   4

Common Core Standard 4.NF.4 – Numbers & Operations – Fractions

☐   Austin had 12 chips on his plate. After eating $\frac{1}{2}$ of them, he gave the remaining chips to his brother Frank. How many chips did Frank get from Austin?

Ⓐ $\frac{1}{24}$ chips   Ⓒ $\frac{13}{2}$ chips

Ⓑ   6 chips   Ⓓ   6.5 chips

Common Core Standard 4.NF.4 – Numbers & Operations – Fractions

☐   Select the correct answer for the following statement:

$$0 \times \frac{2}{3} =$$

Ⓐ $\frac{2}{3}$

Ⓑ   0

Ⓒ   1.5

Ⓓ $\frac{1}{3}$

Name _____   Date_____

Common Core Standard 4.NF.4 – Numbers & Operations – Fractions

☐   If Juanita had 8 shirts to give to charity and she gave $1/4$ of the shirts to her church, how many did she give to her church?

(A) $9/4$ shirts   (C) $1/12$ shirts

(B)   3 shirts   (D)   2 shirts

Common Core Standard 4.NF.4 – Numbers & Operations – Fractions

☐   Select the correct answer for the following statement:

$$18 \times 1/3 =$$

(A) $1/21$

(B)   6

(C)   7

(D) $9/13$

Common Core Standard 4.NF.4 – Numbers & Operations – Fractions

☐   If a glacier moves $1/10$ a mile in one year, how far will it move in 35 years?

(A)   3.6 miles   (C)   3.5 miles

(B) $6/5$ miles   (D) $1/18$ miles

Common Core Standard 4.NF.4 – Numbers & Operations – Fractions

☐   **Select the correct answer for the following statement:**

$$11 \times \frac{1}{8} =$$

Ⓐ $\frac{3}{2}$

Ⓑ   2

Ⓒ $\frac{1}{9}$

Ⓓ   1.375

Common Core Standard 4.NF.4 – Numbers & Operations – Fractions

☐   **Each time the yard is mowed, Tim's lawn mower uses $\frac{3}{5}$ gallons of gas. How much gas is needed to mow the yard 6 times a month?**

Ⓐ   3.6   Ⓒ   1.8

Ⓑ $\frac{3}{11}$ Ⓓ   4

Common Core Standard 4.NF.4 – Numbers & Operations – Fractions

☐   **Select the correct answer for the following statement:**

$$2 \times \frac{11}{12} =$$

Ⓐ $\frac{11}{6}$

Ⓑ $\frac{11}{24}$

Ⓒ $\frac{13}{12}$

Ⓓ $\frac{11}{14}$

Name _____   **Date** _____

☐   **Select the correct answer for the following statement:**

$$\frac{7}{10} \quad + \quad \frac{21}{100} \quad =$$

(A) $\frac{91}{100}$

(B) $\frac{28}{110}$

(C) $\frac{147}{100}$

(D) $\frac{28}{100}$

☐   **Select the correct answer for the following statement:**

$$\frac{61}{100} \quad + \quad \frac{3}{10} \quad =$$

(A) $\frac{64}{100}$

(B) $\frac{64}{110}$

(C) $\frac{91}{100}$

(D) $\frac{183}{100}$

☐   **Select the correct answer for the following statement:**

$$\frac{10}{100} \quad + \quad \frac{2}{10} \quad =$$

(A) $\frac{200}{100}$

(B) $\frac{12}{110}$

(C) $\frac{12}{100}$

(D) $\frac{3}{10}$

Common Core Standard 4.NF.5 – Numbers & Operations – Fractions

☐   **Select the correct answer for the following statement:**

$$\frac{5}{10} \quad + \quad \frac{13}{100} \quad =$$

Ⓐ $\frac{63}{100}$

Ⓑ $\frac{18}{110}$

Ⓒ $\frac{165}{100}$

Ⓓ $\frac{18}{100}$

Common Core Standard 4.NF.5 – Numbers & Operations – Fractions

☐   **Select the correct answer for the following statement:**

$$\frac{47}{100} \quad + \quad \frac{5}{10} \quad =$$

Ⓐ $\frac{52}{100}$

Ⓑ $\frac{52}{110}$

Ⓒ $\frac{97}{100}$

Ⓓ $\frac{235}{100}$

Common Core Standard 4.NF.5 – Numbers & Operations – Fractions

☐   **Select the correct answer for the following statement:**

$$\frac{7}{100} \quad + \quad \frac{9}{10} \quad =$$

Ⓐ $\frac{67}{110}$

Ⓑ $\frac{63}{100}$

Ⓒ $\frac{16}{100}$

Ⓓ $\frac{97}{100}$

Common Core Standard 4.NF.5 – Numbers & Operations – Fractions

☐   **Select the correct answer for the following statement:**

$$^3/_{10} \quad - \quad ^{24}/_{100} \quad =$$

(A) $^{21}/_{90}$

(B) $^3/_{50}$

(C) $^{21}/_{100}$

(D) $^{27}/_{100}$

Common Core Standard 4.NF.5 – Numbers & Operations – Fractions

☐   **Select the correct answer for the following statement:**

$$^2/_{10} \quad - \quad ^{17}/_{100} \quad =$$

(A) $^{19}/_{100}$

(B) $^3/_{100}$

(C) $^{15}/_{90}$

(D) $^{15}/_{100}$

Common Core Standard 4.NF.5 – Numbers & Operations – Fractions

☐   **Select the correct answer for the following statement:**

$$^4/_{10} \quad - \quad ^{39}/_{100} \quad =$$

(A) $^{35}/_{90}$

(B) $^{43}/_{100}$

(C) $^{35}/_{100}$

(D) $^1/_{100}$

Name _____   Date_____

Common Core Standard 4.NF.5 – Numbers & Operations – Fractions

☐   **Select the correct answer for the following statement:**

$$\frac{8}{10} \; - \; \frac{31}{100} \; =$$

(A) $\frac{29}{100}$

(B) $\frac{23}{100}$

(C) $\frac{49}{100}$

(D) $\frac{23}{90}$

Common Core Standard 4.NF.5 – Numbers & Operations – Fractions

☐   **Select the correct answer for the following statement:**

$$\frac{51}{100} \; - \; \frac{5}{10} \; =$$

(A) $\frac{46}{90}$

(B) $\frac{1}{100}$

(C) $\frac{56}{100}$

(D) $\frac{46}{100}$

Common Core Standard 4.NF.5 – Numbers & Operations – Fractions

☐   **Select the correct answer for the following statement:**

$$\frac{80}{100} \; - \; \frac{1}{10} \; =$$

(A) $\frac{79}{90}$

(B) $\frac{81}{100}$

(C) $\frac{7}{10}$

(D) $\frac{79}{100}$

Common Core Standard 4.NF.6 – Numbers & Operations – Fractions

☐ Jonathan played 10 computer games and won 6 of the games or 0.6 when written as a decimal. Which fraction shows the fraction of games he won?

(A) $\frac{4}{10}$

(B) $\frac{6}{4}$

(C) $\frac{4}{6}$

(D) $\frac{6}{10}$

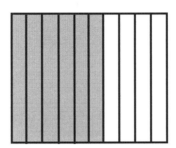

Common Core Standard 4.NF.6 – Numbers & Operations – Fractions

☐ Kamesha's mother bought her 10 new T-shirts for school. Three of the 10, or $\frac{3}{10}$, of the shirts have polka dots. Which is the correct way to write that amount as a decimal?

(A) 0.3

(B) 10.3

(C) 1.03

(D) 0.03

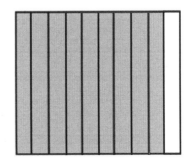

Common Core Standard 4.NF.6 – Numbers & Operations – Fractions

☐ The model is shaded to represent $1\frac{9}{10}$. Which decimal does the model represent?

(A) 1.09

(B) 19.0

(C) 0.19

(D) 1.9

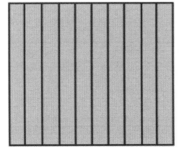

Common Core Standard 4.NF.6 – Numbers & Operations – Fractions

☐ **Which model shows that 0.8 is shaded?**

 Ⓐ

Ⓒ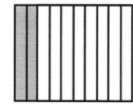

Ⓑ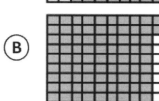

Ⓓ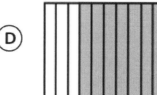

Common Core Standard 4.NF.6 – Numbers & Operations – Fractions

☐ **Lindsey filled a bucket with 2.25 liters of water. Which fraction shows the amount of water she used?**

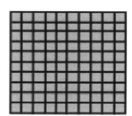

Ⓐ $2\frac{3}{4}$

Ⓒ $1\frac{2}{3}$

Ⓑ $2\frac{1}{4}$

Ⓓ $3\frac{1}{3}$

Common Core Standard 4.NF.6 – Numbers & Operations – Fractions

☐ **Which model shows that 0.32 is shaded?**

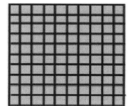 Ⓐ

Ⓒ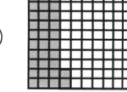

Ⓑ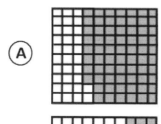

Ⓓ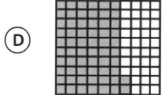

Name _____ Date_____

Common Core Standard 4.NF.6 – Numbers & Operations – Fractions

☐   **Which decimal tells how much is shaded?**

(A)   1.62

(B)   0.162

(C)   162.0

(D)   1.38

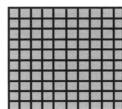

Common Core Standard 4.NF.6 – Numbers & Operations – Fractions

☐   **Russell spent $\frac{65}{100}$ of a dollar for a candy bar. Which tells how much he spent?**

(A) $65.00

(B) $0.65

(C) $6.50

(D) $0.065

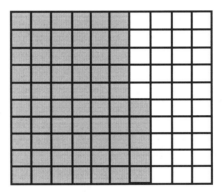

Common Core Standard 4.NF.6 – Numbers & Operations – Fractions

☐   **Runner A and Runner B are having a race. What is the correct way to write the distance of Runner B as a decimal?**

(A)   0.12 mile

(B)   1.20 miles

(C)   0.50 mile

(D)   1.50 miles

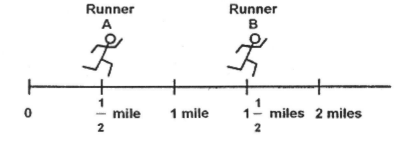

Common Core Standard 4.NF.6 – Numbers & Operations – Fractions

 The model is shaded to represent $1\frac{2}{5}$. Which decimal does the

model represent?

 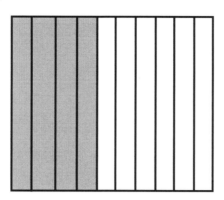 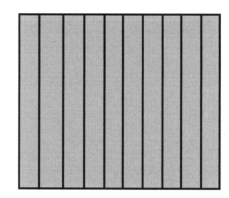

(A) 1.25

(B) 1.4

(C) 0.04

(D) 1.04

Common Core Standard 4.NF.6 – Numbers & Operations – Fractions

 Which model shows that 0.5 is shaded?

(A)

(B)

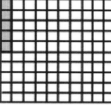

(C)

(D)

Common Core Standard 4.NF.6 – Numbers & Operations – Fractions

 Macey's puppy gained 1.50 pounds last year. What is another way
to write the number of pounds her puppy gained?

(A) $1\frac{15}{100}$ (C) $1\frac{1}{2}$

(B) $1\frac{1}{50}$ (D) $10\frac{100}{50}$

Common Core Standard 4.NF.6 – Numbers & Operations – Fractions

 Which model shows that 0.74 is shaded?

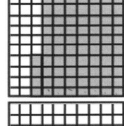

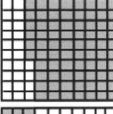
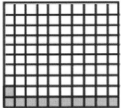

Common Core Standard 4.NF.6 – Numbers & Operations – Fractions

Which decimal tells how much is shaded?

(A) 3.00

(B) 0.003

(C) 0.03

(D) 0.30

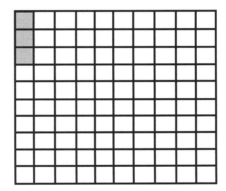

Common Core Standard 4.NF.6 – Numbers & Operations – Fractions

Franklin found $\frac{25}{100}$ of a dollar on the sidewalk and $\frac{79}{100}$ of a dollar under his bed. Which tells the total amount of money he found?

(A) $0.54

(B) $10.40

(C) $0.94

(D) $1.04

Common Core Standard 4.NF.7 – Numbers & Operations – Fractions

☐ **Which problem is true?**

(A) $2.01 = $2.01

(B) $1.77 < $1.77

(C) $1.22 > $1.22

(D) $1.12 = $1.11

Common Core Standard 4.NF.7 – Numbers & Operations – Fractions

☐ **Which answer is correct for the diagrams below?**

(A) =

(B) <

(C) >

(D) ≠

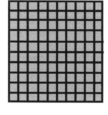
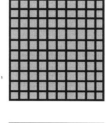
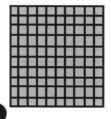
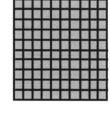
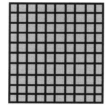
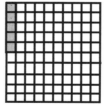

Common Core Standard 4.NF.7 – Numbers & Operations – Fractions

☐ **Which answer is correct for the diagrams below?**

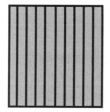
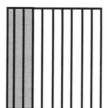

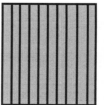

(A) >

(B) =

(C) ≠

(D) <

Common Core Standard 4.NF.7 – Numbers & Operations – Fractions

☐   **Which answer shows the decimals in order from least to greatest?**

4.71   1.63   2.71   1.53

(A)   1.53 < 1.63 < 2.71 < 4.71

(B)   1.63 < 1.53 < 2.71 < 4.71

(C)   1.53 < 1.63 < 4.71 < 2.71

(D)   4.71 < 2.71 < 1.63 < 1.53

Common Core Standard 4.NF.7 – Numbers & Operations – Fractions

☐   **Which decimal is greater than the diagram shown below?**

(A)   0.69

(B)   0.70

(C)   0.60

(D)   0.71

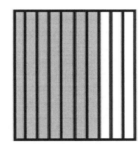

Common Core Standard 4.NF.7 – Numbers & Operations – Fractions

☐   **Look at the sequence of diagrams below, which best describes the pattern?**

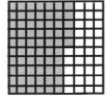 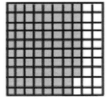 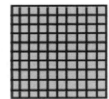

(A)   greatest to least   (C)   least to greatest

(B)   all equal   (D)   not equal

Common Core Standard 4.NF.7 – Numbers & Operations – Fractions

Which answer is correct for the diagrams below?

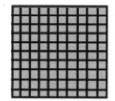 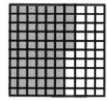 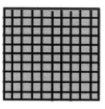 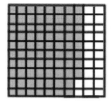

(A) =   (C) <

(B) >   (D) ≠

Common Core Standard 4.NF.7 – Numbers & Operations – Fractions

Which decimal is equal to the diagram shown below?

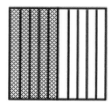

(A) 0.50   (C) 1.50

(B) 0.40   (D) 0.60

Common Core Standard 4.NF.7 – Numbers & Operations – Fractions

Which answer is correct for the decimals below?

0.40 ? 0.19

(A) <

(B) =

(C) >

(D) ≠

Name _____   Date_____

Common Core Standard 4.NF.7 – Numbers & Operations – Fractions

Choose the model that does not represent the greatest number of shaded boxes

(A)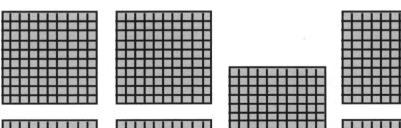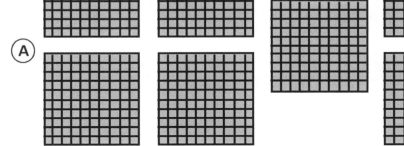

(B)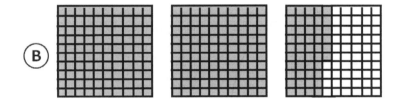

(C)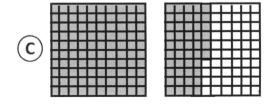

(D)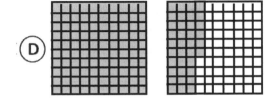

Common Core Standard 4.NF.7 – Numbers & Operations – Fractions

 Choose the model that represent the greatest number of shaded lines.

(A)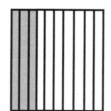

(B)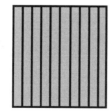

(C)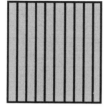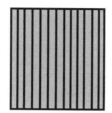

(D)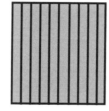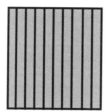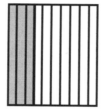

Common Core Standard 4.NF.7 – Numbers & Operations – Fractions

☐   **Which comparison is true for the models below?**

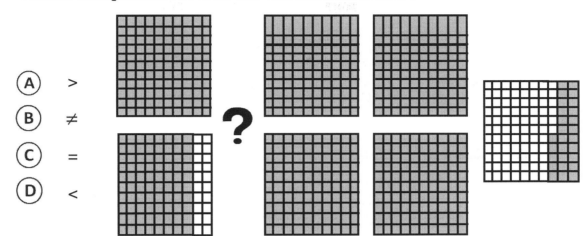

(A)   >

(B)   ≠

(C)   =

(D)   <

Common Core Standard 4.NF.7 – Numbers & Operations – Fractions

☐   **Which comparison is true for the models below?**

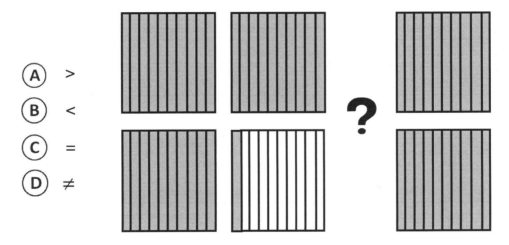

(A)   >

(B)   <

(C)   =

(D)   ≠

Common Core Standard 4.NF.7 – Numbers & Operations – Fractions

☐   **Which comparison is true for the decimals below?**

0.8 **?** 0.1

(A)   =

(B)   <

(C)   >

(D)   ≠

Name _____   Date_____

Common Core Standard 4.MD.1 – Measurement & Data

☐   **Which is the best estimate of the weight of the letter?**

(A) 100 ounces

(B) 3 grams

(C) 30 pounds

(D) 300 tons

Common Core Standard 4.MD.1 – Measurement & Data

☐   **Which of the following objects would most likely be on the scale if the weight of the object is 2 ounces?**

(A) Bag of oranges

(B) Gallon jug of milk

(C) Jelly sandwich

(D) Car

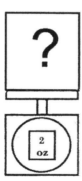

Common Core Standard 4.MD.1 – Measurement & Data

☐   **Which object is most likely to have a mass of 3 grams?**

(A) Envelope

(B) Bicycle

(C) Tomato

(D) Book

Name _____ Date_____

Common Core Standard 4.MD.1 – Measurement & Data

☐   **Which object is most likely to weigh 10 pounds?**

(A)   Car

(B)   Bird

(C)   Paper clip

(D)   Dog

Common Core Standard 4.MD.1 – Measurement & Data

☐   **Which objects are most likely to have a mass of 6 kilograms?**

(A)   Adult man and a cat

(B)   Teenager and a dog

(C)   Ant and a grasshopper

(D)   Rabbit and a cat

Common Core Standard 4.MD.1 – Measurement & Data

☐   **Which is the best estimate of the weight of a bucket of paint?**

(A)   10 pounds

(B)   3 ounces

(C)   40 grams

(D)   10 kilograms

Common Core Standard 4.MD.1 – Measurement & Data

☐   **Which object is most likely to have a mass of 8 ounces?**

(A) Pear

(B) Watermelon

(C) Bicycle

(D) Ruler

Common Core Standard 4.MD.1 – Measurement & Data

☐   **Which is the best estimate of the weight of an adult cat?**

(A) 3 grams

(B) 3 tons

(C) 3 kilograms

(D) 3 ounces

Common Core Standard 4.MD.1 – Measurement & Data

☐   **Which object is most likely to have a weight of 5 kilograms?**

(A) Piece of paper

(B) Bag of oranges

(C) Truck

(D) Pencil

Common Core Standard 4.MD.1 – Measurement & Data

☐   **Which object is most likely to have a capacity of 8 cups?**

(A)   Swimming pool

(B)   Backpack

(C)   Coffeepot

(D)   Pond

Common Core Standard 4.MD.1 – Measurement & Data

☐   **Which container is most likely to have a capacity of 1 cup of water?**

(A)   Container B

(B)   Container C

(C)   Container D

(D)   Container A

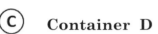

Common Core Standard 4.MD.1 – Measurement & Data

☐   **Which is the best estimate of the amount of water in the bathtub?**

(A)   30 cups

(B)   30 milliliters

(C)   30 liters

(D)   30 gallons

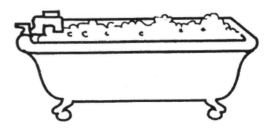

Common Core Standard 4.MD.2 – Measurement & Data

☐ Eve wanted to put ribbon around a basket. The basket is 24 inches long and 6 inches wide. In order to know how much ribbon to buy, Eve must find the perimeter of the basket. Which amount represents the amount of ribbon she must buy?

(A) 30 inches

(B) 40 inches

(C) 18 inches

(D) 60 inches

Common Core Standard 4.MD.2 – Measurement & Data

☐ Miranda gets on the school bus at 7:30 AM. She got up 45 minutes before she got on the bus. What time did she awaken?

(A) 8:15 AM

(B) 6:45 AM

(C) 7:45 AM

(D) 6:15 AM

Common Core Standard 4.MD.2 – Measurement & Data

☐ Bret climbed a tree that is 12 feet 9 inches tall. His brother climbed a tree that is 10 feet 3 inches tall. How much taller was the tree Bret climbed than the tree his brother climbed?

(A) 22 feet 12 inches

(B) 22 feet 6 inches

(C) 2 feet 6 inches

(D) 8 inches

Common Core Standard 4.MD.2 – Measurement & Data

☐ Matthew left school at 3:10 PM to go to a hobby club meeting. The meeting started at 3:30 PM. The meeting lasted 45 minutes. If his mother came to pick him up just as the meeting was ending, what time did she get there?

Ⓐ 3:55 PM

Ⓑ 4:15 PM

Ⓒ 4:00 PM

Ⓓ 4:30 PM

Common Core Standard 4.MD.2 – Measurement & Data

☐ Mary Elizabeth wants to wallpaper one wall in her bedroom. The wall is 9 feet tall and 12 feet long. Her mother also wants a wall in her bedroom wallpapered. Her wall is the same size as the wall in Mary Elizabeth's room. How much wallpaper will she need to complete the both jobs?

Ⓐ 108 sq ft

Ⓑ 21 sq ft

Ⓒ 216 sq ft

Ⓓ 42 sq ft

9 feet

12 feet

Common Core Standard 4.MD.2 – Measurement & Data

☐ Cliff went to a park to play baseball at 9:20. He got home 2 hours and 30 minutes later. What time did he get home?

Ⓐ 11:50

Ⓑ 11:20

Ⓒ 9:50

Ⓓ 11:30

Common Core Standard 4.MD.2 – Measurement & Data

☐   Michael watches his favorite video on Saturday afternoons. It lasts 3 hours. How many minutes does it take for him to watch his video?

(A)   120 min

(B)   180 min

(C)   60 min

(D)   160 min

Common Core Standard 4.MD.2 – Measurement & Data

☐   A fast moving cold front came through Lewisville yesterday morning. At 9:00 AM the temperature was 75° F. By noon it was 19° cooler. At 6:00 PM the temperature had dropped another 6°. What was the temperature at 6:00 PM?

(A)   100° F

(B)   60° F

(C)   50° F

(D)   58° F

Common Core Standard 4.MD.2 – Measurement & Data

☐   Theo did his chores in 1 hour and 52 minutes. His sister did her chores in 125 minutes. How much less time did Theo spend on his chores than his sister?

(A)   237 min

(B)   13 min

(C)   73 min

(D)   65 min

Common Core Standard 4.MD.2 – Measurement & Data

☐ Felipe wanted to watch a movie on the movie channel. The movie was scheduled to be featured every day at noon from August 5 to August 14. If August 11 was a Friday, on which day did the movie begin?

(A) Sunday

(B) Monday

(C) Saturday

(D) Thursday

Common Core Standard 4.MD.2 – Measurement & Data

☐ Brandon came home at 7:15. He had been riding his bicycle for 35 minutes. What time did he begin riding his bicycle?

(A) 7:40

(B) 7:00

(C) 6:40

(D) 6:45

Common Core Standard 4.MD.2 – Measurement & Data

☐ Bill's father is 6 feet 4 inches tall. His mother is 5 feet 3 inches tall. How much taller is his father than his mother?

(A) 11 feet 7 inches

(B) 1 foot 7 inches

(C) 18 inches

(D) 1 foot 1 inch

Common Core Standard 4.MD.2 – Measurement & Data

☐ Angela walks to a library every afternoon after school. It takes her 25 minutes to get from school to the library. If she leaves school at 2:15, what time will she get to the library?

(A) 2:40

(B) 1:50

(C) 2:30

(D) 3:40

Common Core Standard 4.MD.2 – Measurement & Data

☐ Ms. Bivins wants to put a wall hanging on her living room wall. The wall hanging is 4 feet wide and 6 feet long. What is the *area* of the wall that the wall hanging will cover?

(A) 24 sq ft

(B) 10 sq ft

(C) 16 sq ft

(D) 22 sq ft

Common Core Standard 4.MD.2 – Measurement & Data

☐ Brooks and his family went to visit his grandparents last weekend. They arrived at his grandparents' house at 9:25. It took them 3 hours and 45 minutes to make the trip. What time did Brooks and his family leave their home?

(A) 12:70

(B) 6:25

(C) 6:40

(D) 5:40

Name _____ Date _____

Common Core Standard 4.MD.2 – Measurement & Data

☐ **Look at the clocks. Beth's mother jogs every morning before she goes to work. She leaves home at 5:45 and returns at 7:00. How long does it take her to complete her jog?**

(A) 45 minutes

(B) 1 hour 15 minutes

(C) 15 minutes

(D) 2 hours 15 minutes

Start   **Return**

Common Core Standard 4.MD.2 – Measurement & Data

☐ **Jose's basketball game lasted 2 hours. How many minutes did Jose's game last?**

(A) 60 min

(B) 125 min

(C) 90 min

(D) 120 min

Common Core Standard 4.MD.2 – Measurement & Data

☐ **A science class conducted an experiment to see how long it takes an ice cube to melt. The temperature of the ice cube at the beginning of the experiment was 21°F. After 10 minutes, the ice cube's temperature had risen 7°F. At the end of the experiment, the melting ice cube's temperature had risen an additional 9°F. What was the temperature of the ice cube at the end of the experiment?**

(A) 5°F

(B) 37°F

(C) 25°F

(D) 15°F

Common Core Standard 4.MD.3 – Measurement & Data

☐ Amanda's mom wanted Amanda to measure her room to make sure that her new furniture will fit. Amanda measured 12ft as the length of her room and 8ft as the width of it. What would be the area of Amanda's room?

(A) 120 square ft.

(B) 96 square ft.

(C) 86 square ft.

(D) 112 square ft.

Common Core Standard 4.MD.3 – Measurement & Data

☐ A farmer wanted to plant corn on his square field. He measured the perimeter of his field 400yard. What would be the area of farmer's field?

(A) 40,000 sq. ft.

(B) 10,000 ft.

(C) 16,000 sq. ft.

(D) 10,000 sq. ft.

Common Core Standard 4.MD.3 – Measurement & Data

☐ Paul decided to frame the drawing he drew for his mom for Mother's Day. He measured the length of his picture 8in and the width of it 3in more than the length. What would be the perimeter of the frame that Paul needs.

(A) 34 in.

(B) 36 in.

(C) 42 in.

(D) 38 in.

Name _____   Date_____

Common Core Standard 4.MD.3 – Measurement & Data

☐   The city is planning to build a new playground for kids at the
     Woodrow Park. They cleaned up an area of 120sq m. If the length of
     the playground is 12m, what would be the perimeter of the cleaned
     area?

(A)   24 m

(B)   32 m

(C)   44 m

(D)   36 m

Common Core Standard 4.MD.3 – Measurement & Data

☐   What is the area of the shaded figure bellow?

(A)   36 cm

(B)   20 cm

(C)   26sq cm

(D)   20sq cm

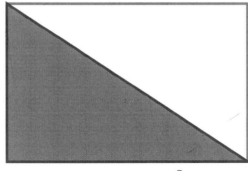

5cm

8cm

Common Core Standard 4.MD.3 – Measurement & Data

☐   Find the area of the figure bellow where N=3cm.

(A)   36 sq. cm

(B)   45 sq. cm

(C)   42 sq. cm

(D)   38 sq. cm

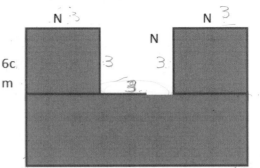

N 3   N 3
                     N
6c   3   3
m   3
              9cm

12 + 18 + 12

54
9
45
6.
24
+ 1.8
72

Common Core Standard 4.MD.3 – Measurement & Data

☐ Lucy runs around the square park every Friday morning at 6:30a.m. How long is the distance of one loop that she runs if the area of the park is 0.25sq km?

(A) 2km

(B) 6km

(C) 4km

(D) 5km

Common Core Standard 4.MD.3 – Measurement & Data

☐ What is the perimeter of a given figure?

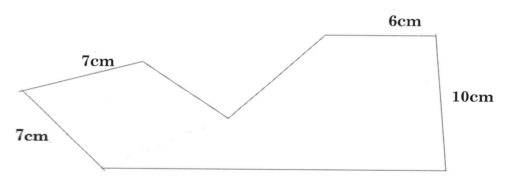

(A) 60 cm

(B) 58 cm

(C) 56 cm

(D) 62 cm

Name _____   Date_____

The perimeter of the rectangle is 70 feet. What is the area of the rectangle?

24feet

(A)   250 square feet   (C)   260 square feet

(B)   244 square feet   (D)   264 square feet

Name _____   Date_____

Common Core Standard 4.MD.4 – Measurement & Data

 Which number line shows the graph of all whole numbers that are greater than 3 *and* less than 6?

(A)

(B)

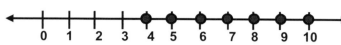

(C)

(D)

Common Core Standard 4.MD.4 – Measurement & Data

Point **Z** best represents what number?

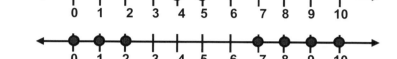

(A) 6.5

(B) 6.7

(C) 6.2

(D) 6.9

Common Core Standard 4.MD.4 – Measurement & Data

Which point on the number line best represents $6\frac{1}{4}$?

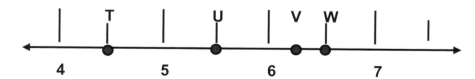

(A) T   (C) W

(B) U   (D) V

Common Core Standard 4.MD.4 – Measurement & Data

☐ Point **S** best represents which number?

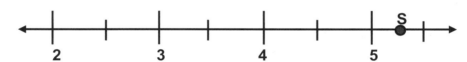

(A) $5\frac{1}{2}$ (C) $6\frac{1}{4}$

(B) $5\frac{1}{4}$ (D) $5\frac{3}{4}$

Common Core Standard 4.MD.4 – Measurement & Data

☐ Which statement describes the graph on the number line below?

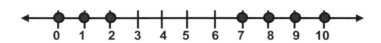

(A) All whole numbers greater than 3 and greater than 6.

(B) All whole numbers less than 7 and greater than 2.

(C) All whole numbers less than 7.

(D) All whole numbers less than 3 and greater than 6.

Common Core Standard 4.MD.4 – Measurement & Data

☐ Point **M** best represents what number?

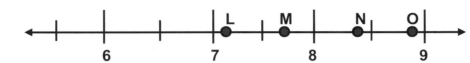

(A) 7.2   (C) 7.7

(B) 7.1   (D) 8.2

Name _____   Date_____

Common Core Standard 4.MD.4 – Measurement & Data

⬜ **Which object on the number line is at a position greater than $\frac{6}{8}$?**

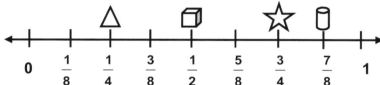

Ⓐ Triangle

Ⓑ Cylinder

Ⓒ Star

Ⓓ Cube

Common Core Standard 4.MD.4 – Measurement & Data

⬜ **Which number line shows the graph of all whole numbers that are less than 8 *and* greater than 5?**

Ⓐ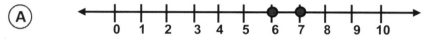

Ⓑ

Ⓒ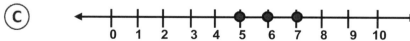

Ⓓ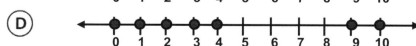

Common Core Standard 4.MD.4 – Measurement & Data

⬜ **Point B best represents what number?**

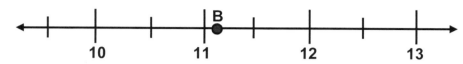

Ⓐ 11.1

Ⓑ 11.6

Ⓒ 11.4

Ⓓ 11.8

Common Core Standard 4.MD.4 – Measurement & Data

☐ **Which point on the number line best represents** $8\frac{3}{4}$?

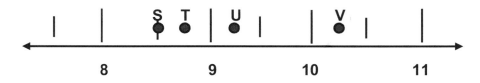

(A) V   (C) S

(B̶) T   (D) U

Common Core Standard 4.MD.4 – Measurement & Data

☐ **Point P best represents which number?**

(A) $14\frac{3}{4}$ (C) $13\frac{1}{4}$

(B) $13\frac{3}{4}$ (D̸) $13\frac{1}{2}$

Common Core Standard 4.MD.4 – Measurement & Data

☐ **Which statement describes the graph on the number line below?**

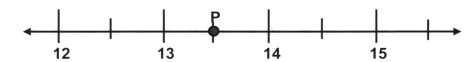

(A) All whole numbers greater than 4.

(B̶) All whole numbers less than 9 and greater than 4.

(C) All whole numbers less than 9.

(D) All whole numbers less than 9 and greater than 5.

Name _____   Date_____

Common Core Standard 4.MD.4 – Measurement & Data

☐   **Point X best represents which number?**

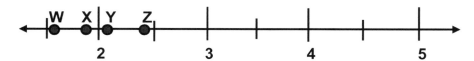

(A)   2.9

(B)   1.6

(C)   2.1

(D)   1.9

Common Core Standard 4.MD.4 – Measurement & Data

☐   **Which object on the number line is at a position greater than $2\frac{4}{6}$?**

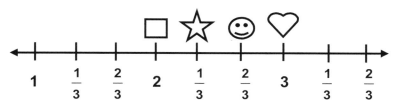

(A)   Face   (C)   Heart

(B)   Star   (D)   Cube

Common Core Standard 4.MD.4 – Measurement & Data

☐   **An inchworm is racing along a number line. Which number tells how far the inchworm has gone?**

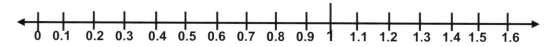

(A)   1

(B)   1.2

(C)   0.8

(D)   2

Common Core Standard 4.MD.4 – Measurement & Data

☐   **Which number line shows the graph of all whole numbers that are greater than 0 _and_ less than 5?**

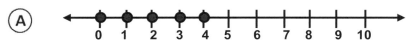

Common Core Standard 4.MD.4 – Measurement & Data

☐   **Point Y best represents what number?**

(A)   17.7

(B)   17.1

(C)   17.3

(D)   17.5

Common Core Standard 4.MD.4 – Measurement & Data

☐   **Point E best represents which number?**

(A) $3\frac{1}{2}$ (C) $3\frac{1}{4}$

(B) $3\frac{3}{4}$ (D) $4\frac{1}{4}$

Name _____   Date_____

Common Core Standard 4.MD.4 – Measurement & Data

☐   **Which statement describes the graph on the number line below?**

(A)   All whole numbers greater than 1 and less than 6.

(B)   All whole numbers less than 5 and greater than 2.

(C)   All whole numbers less than 6.

(D)   All whole numbers greater than 2 and less than 5.

Common Core Standard 4.MD.4 – Measurement & Data

☐   **Point O best represents which number?**

(A)   5.9

(B)   4.9

(C)   4.6

(D)   4.4

Common Core Standard 4.MD.4 – Measurement & Data

☐   **Which object on the number line is at a position less than $1\frac{2}{4}$?**

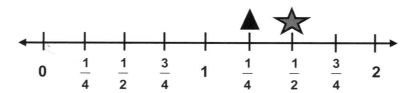

(A)   Star   (C)   Book

(B)   Key   (D)   Triangle

Common Core Standard 4.MD.4 – Measurement & Data

☐   **Which letter is located on point 1.3?**

(A)   U   (C)   N

(B)   T   (D)   I

Common Core Standard 4.MD.5 – Measurement & Data

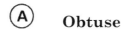 What kind of angle has been formed by these two rays that share point A?

(A)   Obtuse

(B)   Straight

(C)   Acute

(D)   Right

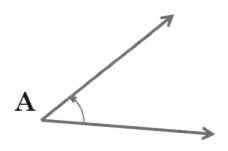

Common Core Standard 4.MD.5 – Measurement & Data

What angle is formed by the two rays at their crossing point X?

(A)   Acute

(B)   Right

(C)   Straight

(D)   Obtuse

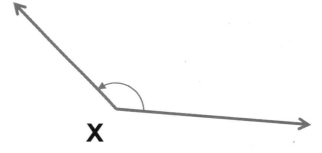

Common Core Standard 4.MD.5 – Measurement & Data

What kind of angle is this?

(A)   Acute

(B)   Right

(C)   Straight

(D)   Obtuse

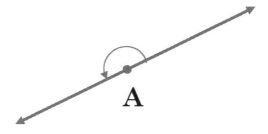

Common Core Standard 4.MD.5 – Measurement & Data

☐ **What answer most accurately describes the angle that primary direction lines form on the compass rose below?**

Ⓐ Parallel

Ⓑ Perpendicular

Ⓒ Intersecting

Ⓓ None

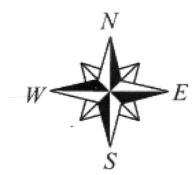

Common Core Standard 4.MD.5 – Measurement & Data

☐ **What is an angle between the hour and minute hands of a clock at 3 o'clock?**

Ⓐ 45°

Ⓑ 180°

Ⓒ 90°

Ⓓ 270°

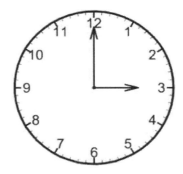

Common Core Standard 4.MD.5 – Measurement & Data

☐ **Which answer most accurately describes the figure shown?**

Ⓐ Parallel lines

Ⓑ Perpendicular lines

Ⓒ Intersecting lines

Ⓓ None

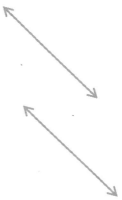

Common Core Standard 4.MD.5 – Measurement & Data

☐   **Which 2 angles could be put together to form an acute angle?**

A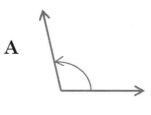

C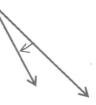

B

D

Ⓐ **Angles C and D**   Ⓒ **Angles A and C**

Ⓑ **Angles B and C**   Ⓓ **Angles B and D**

Common Core Standard 4.MD.5 – Measurement & Data

☐   **What fraction of a turn this angle is equal to?**

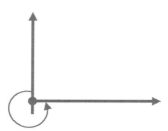

Ⓐ 1/2   Ⓒ 3/4

Ⓑ 1/4   Ⓓ 1

Common Core Standard 4.MD.5 – Measurement & Data

☐   **What fraction does the turn below represents?**

Ⓐ 1/2

Ⓑ 3/4

Ⓒ 1

Ⓓ 1/4

Common Core Standard 4.MD.5 – Measurement & Data

☐   **What kind of angles does this hexagon have?**

(A)   All acute

(B)   All straight

(C)   All right

(D)   All obtuse

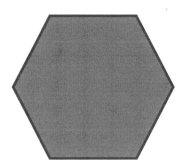

Common Core Standard 4.MD.5 – Measurement & Data

☐   **What kind of angle is angle D?**

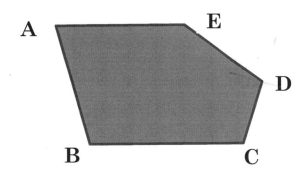

(A)   Acute   (C)   Obtuse

(B)   Right   (D)   Straight

Common Core Standard 4.MD.6 – Measurement & Data

☐   **Which angle describes the angle shown on the protractor?**

 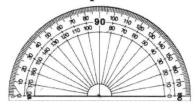

(A)   Acute angle of #

(B)   Obtuse angle of #

(C)   Acute angle of

(D)   Obtuse angle of

Common Core Standard 4.MD.6 – Measurement & Data

☐   **Use a protractor to measure the angle bellow.**

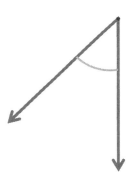

(A) 40°   (C) 34°

(B) 57°   (D) 45°

Common Core Standard 4.MD.6 – Measurement & Data

☐   **Use a protractor to measure the angle bellow.**

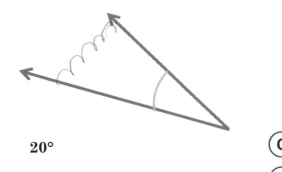

(A)   20°   (C)   35°

(B)   28°   (D)   33°

Common Core Standard 4.MD.6 – Measurement & Data

☐   **Use a protractor to measure the angle between these arrows.**

(A)   165°

(B)   169°

(C)   159°

(D)   155°

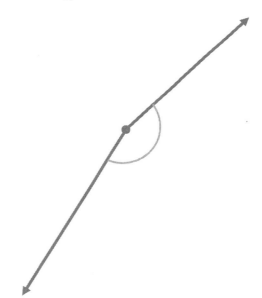

Name _____   Date_____

☐   Use your protractor to measure all the angles in this triangle.

Ⓐ   90° 25° 65°

Ⓑ   90° 45° 45°

Ⓒ   90° 35° 55°

Ⓓ   90° 10° 80°

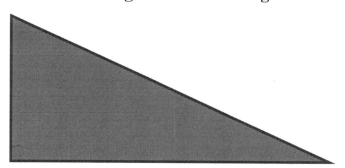

☐   What is an angle between the hands of a clock at 1 o'clock?

Ⓐ   90°

Ⓑ   45°

Ⓒ   30°

Ⓓ   25°

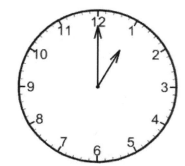

☐   What is an angle between the hands of a clock at 2 o'clock?

Ⓐ   90°

Ⓑ   30°

Ⓒ   60°

Ⓓ   45°

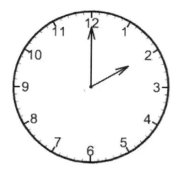

Common Core Standard 4.MD.7 – Measurement & Data

☐   **What is the sum of the two angles WXY and YXZ bellow?**

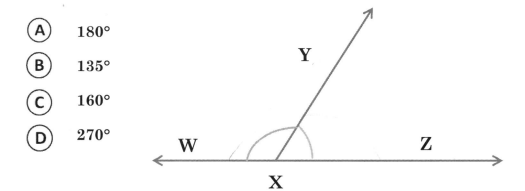

(A)   180°

(B)   135°

(C)   160°

(D)   270°

Common Core Standard 4.MD.7 – Measurement & Data

☐   **What is the sum of the angles shown on the picture bellow?**

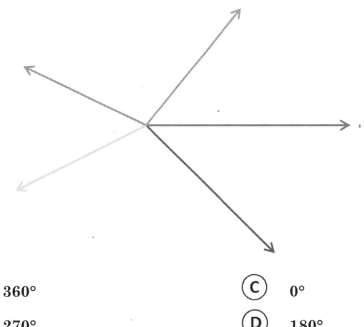

(A)   360°   (C)   0°

(B)   270°   (D)   180°

Common Core Standard 4.MD.7 – Measurement & Data

☐   **What is the measure of angles?**

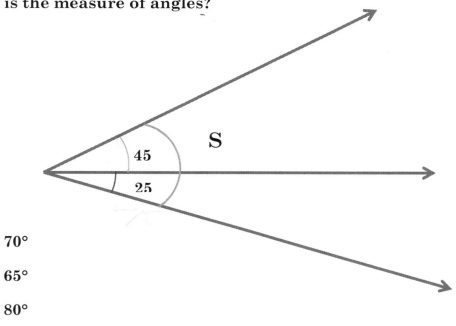

S

45

25

(A)   70°

(B)   65°

(C)   80°

(D)   50°

Common Core Standard 4.MD.7 – Measurement & Data

☐   **Calculate angle P.**

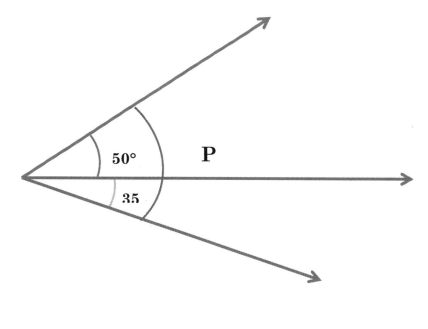

50°

P

35

(A)   75°

(B)   90°

(C)   85°

(D)   80°

Common Core Standard 4.MD.7 – Measurement & Data

☐   **Calculate the angle ABC.**

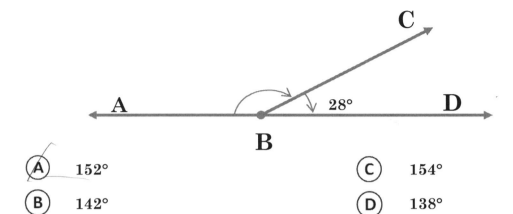

(A)   152°   (C)   154°

(B)   142°   (D)   138°

Common Core Standard 4.G.1 – Geometry

☐   **What angle is formed when perpendicular lines meet?**

Ⓐ̶   **Right**

Ⓑ   **Straight**

Ⓒ   **Obtuse**

Ⓓ   **Acute**

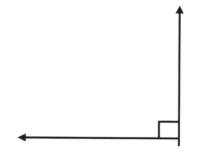

Common Core Standard 4.G.1 – Geometry

☐   **Which pair of angles could you put together to form a right angle?**

Ⓐ   **B**

Ⓑ   **D**

Ⓒ   **C**

Ⓓ   **A**

Common Core Standard 4.G.1 – Geometry

☐   **Look at the drawing of the desk. Based on the drawing, the top of the desk *appears* to be made up of which of the following angles?**

Ⓐ   **Right angles only**

Ⓑ   **Right and obtuse angles**

Ⓒ   **Right and acute angles**

Ⓓ   **Acute and obtuse angles**

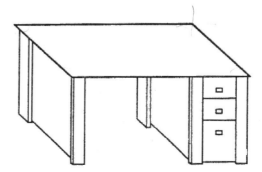

Name _____   Date_____

Common Core Standard 4.G.1 – Geometry

☐   **Look at the angles. Which of the following is the *greatest* angle?**

(A) C

(B) B

(C) D

(D) A

A

C

B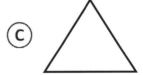

D

Common Core Standard 4.G.1 – Geometry

☐   **Which triangle has an obtuse angle?**

(A)

(B)

(C)

(D)

Common Core Standard 4.G.1 – Geometry

☐   **Which kind of angles form a square?**

(A) Obtuse

(B) Right

(C) Straight

(D) Acute

Common Core Standard 4.G.1 – Geometry

☐   **Look at the telescope and the angle it forms. What kind of angle is formed beneath the telescope?**

(A)   **Obtuse**

(B)   **Right**

(C)   **Acute**

(D)   **Straight**

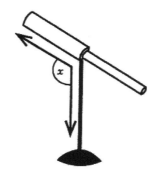

Common Core Standard 4.G.1 – Geometry

☐   **Highway 28 and Highway 3 meet to form which kind of an angle?**

(A)   **Straight**

(B)   **Obtuse**

(C)   **Acute**

(D)   **Right**

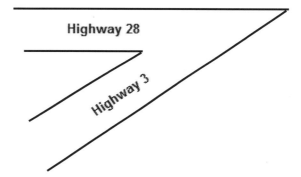

Common Core Standard 4.G.1 – Geometry

☐   **Which 2 angles could be put together to form an obtuse angle?**

(A)   **Angles A and B**

(B)   **Angles B and D**

(C)   **Angles A and C**

(D)   **Angles A and D**

Common Core Standard 4.G.1 – Geometry

☐   The shelf is made up of 6 sections. Which of the following is an angle found in one of the sections of the shelf?

(A)   Obtuse angle only

(B)   Right angle only

(C)   Right and obtuse angles

(D)   Acute angle only

Common Core Standard 4.G.1 – Geometry

☐   Look at the angles. Which of the following is the *least* angle?

(A)   Angle B

(B)   Angle A

(C)   Angle D

(D)   Angle C

A

C

B

D

Common Core Standard 4.G.1 – Geometry

☐   Which of the angles represents an obtuse angle?

(A)   Angle C

(B)   Angle B

(C)   Angle A

(D)   Angle D

A

C

B

D

Common Core Standard 4.G.1 – Geometry

☐   In the closed figure below, which angle is a right angle?

Ⓐ 5

Ⓑ 1

Ⓒ 3

Ⓓ 2

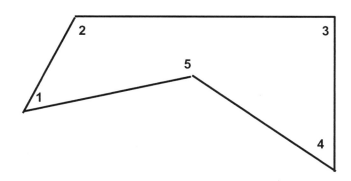

Common Core Standard 4.G.1 – Geometry

☐   Look at the hands on each clock. Which clock's hands form an obtuse angle?

Ⓐ C

Ⓑ B

Ⓒ D

Ⓓ A

Common Core Standard 4.G.1 – Geometry

☐   Look at the arrow on the inside of the letter "**V**". Which kind of angle do the legs of the letter "**V**" form?

Ⓐ Obtuse

Ⓑ Right

Ⓒ Straight

Ⓓ Acute

Common Core Standard 4.G.1 – Geometry

☐   **Which 2 angles could be put together to form an acute angle?**

Ⓐ   **Angle C and D**

Ⓑ   **Angle B and C**

Ⓒ   **Angle A and C**

Ⓓ   **Angle B and D**

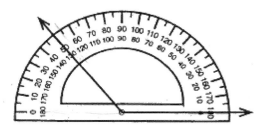

Common Core Standard 4.G.1 – Geometry

☐   **Which correctly describes the angle shown on the protractor?**

Ⓐ   **Acute angle of 50°**   Ⓒ   **Obtuse angle of 130°**

Ⓑ   **Obtuse angle of 50°**   Ⓓ   **Acute angle of 130°**

Common Core Standard 4.G.1 – Geometry

☐   **Which of the angles is greater than a right angle?**

Ⓐ   **Angle A**

Ⓑ   **Angle B**

Ⓒ   **Angle D**

Ⓓ   **Angle C**

Name _____   Date_____

Common Core Standard 4.G.1 – Geometry

□   **Which best describes the angle formed by the lawn chair?**

(A)   **Acute**

(B)   **Right**

(C)   **Obtuse**

(D)   **Straight**

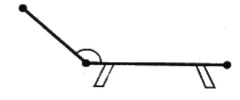

Common Core Standard 4.G.2 – Geometry

☐   Look at the cereal box. How many faces does a rectangular prism have?

(A)   8

(B)   6

(C)   4

(D)   2

Common Core Standard 4.G.2 – Geometry

☐   Which figure represents a triangular prism?

(A)   B

(B)   C

(C)   A

(D)   D

 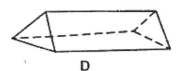

Common Core Standard 4.G.2 – Geometry

☐   Home plate on a baseball field has 5 sides. The figure formed by the home plate is a ———— .

(A)   Hexagon

(B)   Rhombus

(C)   Pentagon

(D)   Octagon

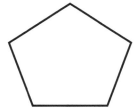

Common Core Standard 4.G.2 – Geometry

☐   **Which figure will be formed when points A, B, C, and A are connected in order by line segments?**

(A) Rectangle

(B) Pentagon

(C) Triangle

(D) Square

A
●

● B

●
C

Common Core Standard 4.G.2 – Geometry

☐   **How many edges does a cube have?**

(A) 12

(B) 6

(C) 4

(D) 8

Common Core Standard 4.G.2 – Geometry

☐   **I am a solid figure that has no faces, no vertices, and no edges. What am I?**

(A) Cube

(B) Sphere

(C) Rectangular prism

(D) Cone

Common Core Standard 4.G.2 – Geometry

☐   **Which figure has exactly 5 faces?**

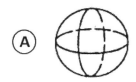

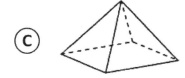

(A)   (C)

(B)   (D)

Common Core Standard 4.G.2 – Geometry

☐   **Which solid figure would match this net?**

(A)   **Rectangular prism**

(B)   **Cube**

(C)   **Sphere**

(D)   **Square pyramid**

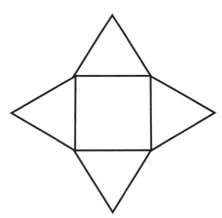

Common Core Standard 4.G.2 – Geometry

☐   **Which figure has the *greatest* number of vertices?**

(A)   C

(B)   B

(C)   D

(D)   A

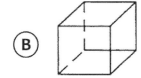

A

B

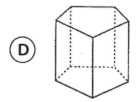

C

D

Common Core Standard 4.G.2 – Geometry

☐   **Which figure best represents a rectangular prism?**

(A) A

(B) C

(C) D

(D) B

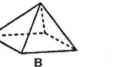

Common Core Standard 4.G.2 – Geometry

☐   **How many sides does the figure below have?**

(A) 3

(B) 1

(C) 0

(D) 4

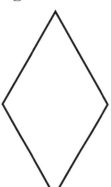

Common Core Standard 4.G.2 – Geometry

☐   **Which figure will be formed when points D, E, F, G, H, I, J, K, and D are connected in order by line segments?**

(A) Rectangle

(B) Octagon

(C) Pentagon

(D) Hexagon

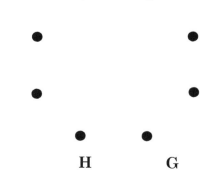

Common Core Standard 4.G.2 – Geometry

☐   How many edges does a triangular prism have?

(A) 4

(B) 8

(C) 2

(D) 3

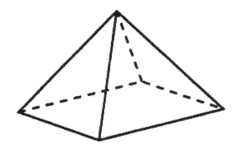

Common Core Standard 4.G.2 – Geometry

☐   If you unfold a cube, which net would it look like?

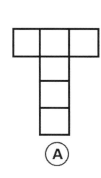
(A)

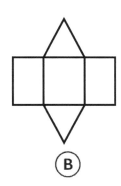
(B)

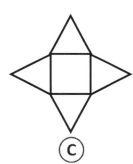
(C)

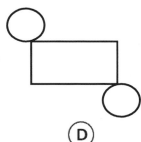
(D)

Common Core Standard 4.G.2 – Geometry

☐   What is the total number of vertices on the figure?

(A) 12

(B) 6

(C) 4

(D) 8

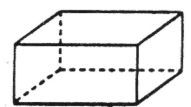

Common Core Standard 4.G.2 – Geometry

☐   **How many faces does this sphere have?**

(A) 4

(B) 8

(C) 0

(D) 3

Common Core Standard 4.G.2 – Geometry

☐   **How many sides does the figure below have?**

(A) 6

(B) 1

(C) 5

(D) 0

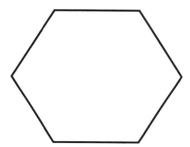

Common Core Standard 4.G.2 – Geometry

☐   **Which figure will be formed when points A, B, C, D, E, and A are connected in order by line segments?**

(A) Octagon

(B) Triangle

(C) Hexagon

(D) Pentagon

Common Core Standard 4.G.2 – Geometry

☐   **How many edges does this figure have?**

(A)   4

(B)   0

(C)   1

(D)   2

Common Core Standard 4.G.2 – Geometry

☐   **I am a solid figure that has 6 faces, 8 vertices, and 12 edges. What am I?**

(A)   Cube

(B)   Square pyramid

(C)   Sphere

(D)   Cylinder

Common Core Standard 4.G.3 – Geometry

☐   **Which figure has only 1 line of symmetry?**

Ⓐ

Ⓒ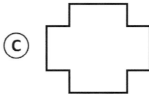

Ⓑ

Ⓓ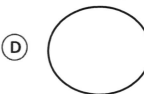

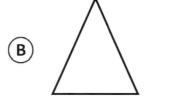

Common Core Standard 4.G.3 – Geometry

☐   **Which letter has a line of symmetry?**

Ⓐ **J**

Ⓑ **Q**

Ⓒ **P**

Ⓓ **B**

Common Core Standard 4.G.3 – Geometry

☐   **Which letter has 2 lines of symmetry?**

Ⓐ **V**

Ⓑ **T**

Ⓒ **H**

Ⓓ **C**

Common Core Standard 4.G.3 – Geometry

[ ]   **Which does NOT show a figure with a line of symmetry?**

Ⓐ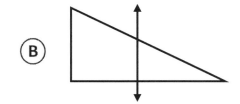

Ⓒ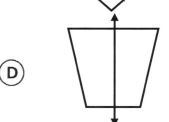

Ⓑ

Ⓓ

Common Core Standard 4.G.3 – Geometry

[ ]   **Which figure shows a line of symmetry?**

Ⓐ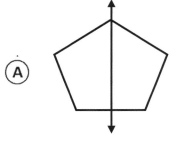

Ⓒ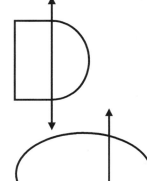

Ⓑ

Ⓓ

Common Core Standard 4.G.3 – Geometry

[ ]   **Which letter does NOT have a line of symmetry?**

Ⓐ **Y**

Ⓑ **D**

Ⓒ **G**

Ⓓ **E**

Common Core Standard 4.G.3 – Geometry

☐   **Which number has at least one line of symmetry?**

(A) **6**

(B) **5**

(C) **3**

(D) **4**

Common Core Standard 4.G.3 – Geometry

☐   **Which figure has more than 1 line of symmetry?**

(A)

(C)

(B)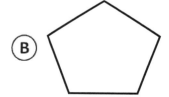

(D)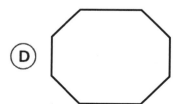

Common Core Standard 4.G.3 – Geometry

☐   **Which does NOT show a figure with a line of symmetry?**

(A)

(C)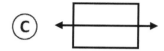

(B)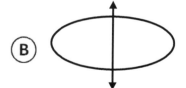

(D)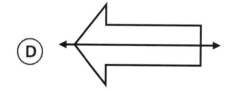

Common Core Standard 4.G.3 – Geometry

☐   **Which figure shows a line of symmetry?**

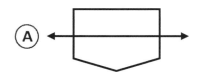

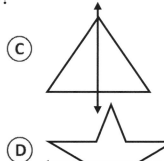

Common Core Standard 4.G.3 – Geometry

☐   **Which number does NOT have a line of symmetry?**

(A) **8**

(B) **7**

(C) **3**

(D) **0**

Common Core Standard 4.G.3 – Geometry

☐   **Which letter has only 1 line of symmetry?**

(A) **I**

(B) **H**

(C) **X**

(D) **C**

Common Core Standard 4.G.3 – Geometry

☐   **Which number has 2 lines of symmetry?**

Ⓐ **8**

Ⓑ **3**

Ⓒ **9**

Ⓓ **4**

Common Core Standard 4.G.3 – Geometry

☐   **Which number has only 1 line of symmetry?**

Ⓐ **4**

Ⓑ **8**

Ⓒ **3**

Ⓓ **0**

Common Core Standard 4.G.3 – Geometry

☐   **Which figure has a line of symmetry?**

Ⓐ

Ⓒ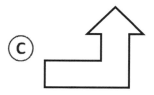

Ⓑ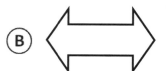

Ⓓ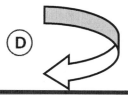

Common Core Standard 4.G.3 – Geometry

☐   **Which letter does NOT have a line of symmetry?**

Ⓐ **V**

Ⓑ **T**

Ⓒ **B**

Ⓓ **J**

Common Core Standard 4.G.3 – Geometry

☐   **Which does NOT show a figure with a line of symmetry?**

Ⓐ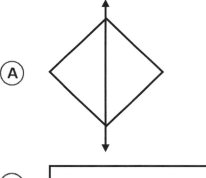

Ⓒ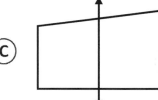

Ⓑ

Ⓓ

Common Core Standard 4.G.3 – Geometry

☐   **Which figure shows a line of symmetry?**

Ⓐ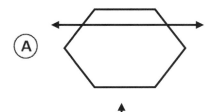

Ⓒ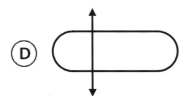

Ⓑ

Ⓓ

Common Core Standard 4.G.3 – Geometry

☐   **Which is a pair of figures that are NOT congruent?**

(A) 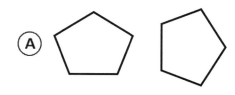   (C)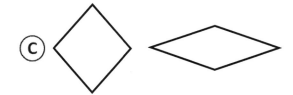

(B)    (D)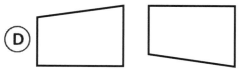

Common Core Standard 4.G.3 – Geometry

☐   **Which 2 figures are congruent?**

(A) 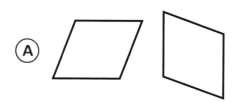   (C)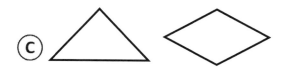

(B)    (D)

Common Core Standard 4.G.3 – Geometry

☐   **Which pair of figures appears to be congruent?**

(A) **1 and 3**

(B) **3 and 7**

(C) **2 and 6**

(D) **1 and 7**

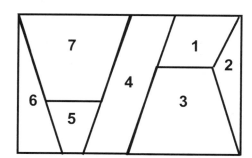

Common Core Standard 4.G.3 – Geometry

☐   **Which figure is NOT congruent to the other 3 figures?**

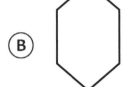
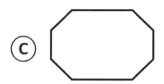
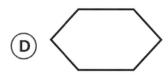

Common Core Standard 4.G.3 – Geometry

☐   **Which grid does NOT contain a pair of congruent figures?**

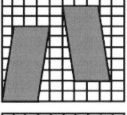

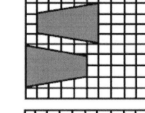

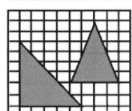
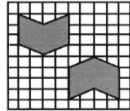

Common Core Standard 4.G.3 – Geometry

☐   **Which 2 shapes are congruent?**

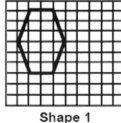
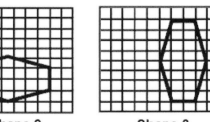
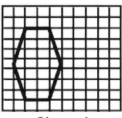

Shape 1   Shape 2   Shape 3   Shape 4

Ⓐ   **Shapes 2 and 4**   Ⓒ   **Shapes 3 and 4**

Ⓑ   **Shapes 1 and 3**   Ⓓ   **Shapes 1 and 4**

ANSWER KEY

4.OA.1

Page 1 .... A, C, D

Page 2 .... B, A, C

Page 3 .... D, C, A

Page 4 .... C, D, B

Page 5 .... A, C, D

Page 6 .... D, B, C

4.OA.2

Page 7 .... C, D, B

Page 8 .... C, B, D

Page 9 .... C, B, D

Page 10 .... B, C, D

Page 11 .... C, B, C

Page 12 .... D, B, A

4.OA.3

Page 13 .... C, A, B

Page 14 .... D, C, A

Page 15 .... B, D, C

Page 16 .... B, D, B

Page 17 .... A, B, C

Page 18 .... B, A, C

4.OA.4

Page 19 .... C, D, C

Page 20 .... C, A, B

Page 21 .... D, B , A

Page 22 .... C, A, B

Page 23 .... C, A, D

4.OA.5

Page 24 .... B, C, D

Page 25 .... A, C, B

Page 26 .... C, B, D

Page 27 .... D, B, C

Page 28 .... C, B, D

4.NBT.1

Page 29 .... D, B

Page 30 .... B, D, B

Page 31 .... A, B, C

Page 32 .... A, A, C

Page 33 .... A

4.NBT.2

Page 34 .... C, D, B

Page 35 .... D, A, C

Page 36 .... C, B, A

Page 37 .... B, C, A

Page 38 .... D, B, C

Page 39 .... D, C, A

4.NBT.3

Page 40 .... D, C, B

Page 83 .... D, A, D

Page 84 .... A, B, C

Page 85 .... A, B, D

Page 86 .... B, D, C

Page 87 .... A, C, D

4.NF.7

Page 88 .... A, C, D

Page 89 .... A, D, C

Page 90 .... B, A, C

Page 91 .... D

Page 92 .... D

Page 93 .... D, B, C

4.MD.1

Page 94 .... B, C, A

Page 95 .... D, D, A

Page 96 .... A, C, B

Page 97 .... C, B, D

4.MD.2

Page 98 .... D, B, C

Page 99 .... B, C, A

Page 100 .... B, C, B

Page 101 .... C, C, D

Page 102 .... A, A, D

Page 103 .... B, D, B

4.MD.3

Page 104 .... B, D, D

Page 105 .... C, D, B

Page 106 .... A, A

Page 107 .... D

4.MD.4

Page 108 .... C, B, D

Page 109 .... B, D, C

Page 110 .... B, D, A

Page 111 .... B, D, B

Page 112 .... D, C, B

Page 113 .... D, D, B

Page 114 .... A, B, D

Page 115 C

4.MD.5

Page 116 .... C, D, C

Page 117 .... B, C, A

Page 118 .... A, C, C

Page 119 .... D, B

4.MD.6

Page 120 .... D, D

Page 121 .... B, A

Page 122 .... A

4.MD.7

Page 123 .... C, C, A

Page 124 .... A, A

Page 125 .... C, A

4.G.1

4.G.2

4.G.3

Made in the USA
San Bernardino, CA
15 September 2013